ON THE COVER
Cover: Larch trees on McGregor Mountain, Stephen Mather Wilderness, North Cascades National Park, Washington
Photography by: NPS/Keith Brumund-Smith

Conserving Natural Resources in the National Parks
Fiscal Year 2011 Report to Congress

Natural Resource Report NPS/NRSS/NRR—2012/541

National Park Service
Natural Resource Stewardship and Science
1201 Oakridge Drive, Suite 150
Fort Collins, CO 80525

June 2012

U.S. Department of the Interior
National Park Service
Natural Resource Stewardship and Science
Fort Collins, Colorado

The National Park Service Natural Resource Stewardship and Science office in Fort Collins, Colorado, publishes a range of reports that address natural resource topics of interest and applicability to a broad audience in the National Park Service and others in natural resource management, including scientists, conservation and environmental constituencies, and the public.

The Natural Resource Report Series is used to disseminate high-priority, current natural resource management information with managerial application. The series targets a general, diverse audience, and may contain NPS policy considerations or address sensitive issues of management applicability.

All manuscripts in the series receive the appropriate level of peer review to ensure that the information is scientifically credible, technically accurate, appropriately written for the intended audience, and designed and published in a professional manner.

Views, statements, findings, conclusions, recommendations, and data in this report do not necessarily reflect views and policies of the National Park Service, U.S. Department of the Interior. Mention of trade names or commercial products does not constitute endorsement or recommendation for use by the U.S. Government.

This report is available from http://www.nature.nps.gov/challenge/reportstocongress.cfm and the Natural Resource Publications Management Web site (http://www.nature.nps.gov/publications/nrpm/) on the Internet.

Please cite this publication as:
National Park Service. 2012. Conserving natural resources in national parks: Fiscal year 2011 report to Congress. Natural Resource Report NPS/NRSS/NRR—2012/541. National Park Service, Fort Collins, Colorado.

NPS 909/115244, June 2012

Contents

Chapter 1: Introduction 1
Measuring Progress 1

Chapter 2: Natural Resource Programs 3
Parks and Regions 3
Network Programs 3
   Cooperative Ecosystem Studies Units 3
   Exotic Plant Management Teams 5
   Inventory and Monitoring Networks 5
   Research Learning Centers 9
Servicewide Natural Resource Programs 11
   Air Quality 11
   Biological Resource Management 12
   Climate Change Response 13
   Environmental Quality 14
   Geologic Resources 15
   Natural Sounds and Night Skies 16
   Social Science 17
   Water Resources 18
Natural Resource Projects 20

Chapter 3: Accomplishments by Region 23
Alaska Region 23
Intermountain Region 26
Midwest Region 30
National Capital Region 34
Northeast Region 38
Pacific West Region 41
Southeast Region 45

Chapter 4: Servicewide Accomplishments 49

Appendixes
A Natural Resource Challenge Funding in Parks 53
B Natural Resource Program Funding–Servicewide Programs 54
C Biological Resource Management Competitive Projects 59
D Climate Change Response Program Projects 60
E Natural Sounds Projects 63
F Water Resource Program Projects 64
G Resource Protection (RP) Projects 68
H Natural Resource Preservation Program Projects 69
I Park-Oriented Biological Support Projects 79

Indexes
Park Index 81
State and Territory Index 84

Chapter 1: Introduction

In August 2011 the National Park Service (NPS) launched *A Call to Action: Preparing for a Second Century of Stewardship and Engagement*, a long-term strategy that marries the fundamental mission of the Service with short- and long-term resource stewardship. The Service has worked tirelessly to preserve parks since its establishment in 1916, but today's challenges require a new, cooperative strategy that takes advantage of state-of-the-art tools and technology. The strategic plan defines a vision for NPS preservation, conservation, and restoration and identifies actions that advance the Service toward that shared vision.

As the National Park Service approaches its second century, it will address four themes: connecting people to parks, advancing the education mission, preserving America's special places, and enhancing professional and organizational excellence. Attaining this vision requires increased partnership and citizen participation in all areas, including park science and stewardship. Natural resource programs across the National Park System continue to be critical to successfully achieving the *Call to Action* vision as well as the vision described in America's Great Outdoors.

For example, the NPS Migration Conservation Initiative is working with the national and international science community not only to identify migration corridors for species that make annual treks from breeding grounds to wintering areas but also to protect the very phenomenon of migration (ACTION 22: SCALING UP). The Inventory and Monitoring Program is developing "state of the park" reports to assess the overall status and condition of natural and cultural resources, park facilities, and visitor satisfaction. The reports will be used to help parks set priorities and communicate complex information about a park's condition to the public in a clear and simple way (ACTION 28: PARK PULSE). The Natural Sounds and Night Skies Program is leading the way to protect natural darkness as a precious resource through development of a service-wide night sky inventory (ACTION 27: STARRY, STARRY NIGHT).

Cascades Climate Challenge, North Cascades National Park, Washington
NPS PHOTO

Natural resource programs are able to take on such complex initiatives because of the solid foundation established by the Natural Resource Challenge ("the Challenge"). Launched in 1999, the Challenge made science-based management of natural resources a top priority, thereby preparing the Service to address 21st-century challenges. The Report to Congress describes natural resource activities across the National Park System in Fiscal Year 2011. By doing so, it responds to a request from Congress that the National Park Service report on Challenge-related expenditures and accomplishments.

Whether engaging youth and citizen scientists and discovering new species through biodiversity discovery events; preserving park resources and viewsheds while addressing alternative energy development; conserving North America's largest land mammal, the American bison; or protecting dark night skies and natural sounds, the National Park Service is taking action to ensure that the nation's natural and cultural heritage persist well into the future. This is not only the National Park Service's responsibility, but also the nation's gift to the American people and people of the world.

Measuring Progress

The National Park Service uses performance goals to measure the effectiveness of its programs. These goals are outlined in the Department of the Interior's *Strategic Plan for Fiscal Years 2011–2016*, which was established in accordance with the Government Performance and Results Act (GPRA) of 1993. Fiscal Year 2011 strategic plan targets and results are available in *Budget Justifications and Performance Information, Fiscal Year 2013* (pages 16–17).

Chapter 2: Natural Resource Programs

The natural resource program in the National Park Service operates on park, regional, network, and servicewide levels. This chapter describes natural resources programs and FY 2011 highlights. More detailed accomplishments representative of the many natural resource activities across the National Park System can be found in Chapters 3 and 4.

The work of the natural resource programs contributes directly to the *Call to Action* goals of preserving America's special places by managing the natural and cultural resources of the National Park System to increase resilience in the face of climate change and other stressors; cultivating excellence in science and scholarship as a foundation for park planning, policy, decision making, and education; achieving a standard of excellence in cultural and natural resource stewardship that serves as a model throughout the world; and collaborating with other land managers and partners to create, restore, and maintain landscape-scale connectivity. In addition, some activities address the remaining *Call to Action* themes of connecting people to parks, advancing the education mission, and enhancing professional excellence. Where programs contribute to a specific action, that item is identified in the text.

Parks and Regions

Parks form the core of the natural resource management effort. Scientists and resource managers practice the natural resource stewardship cycle of discovery, learning, understanding, sharing, protecting, restoring, and evaluating at park and regional scales. Thirty-six parks received base increases from the Challenge, which increased their capacity to deal with threats to natural resources (see Appendix A for natural resource funding in these parks). Regional programs also benefitted from the Challenge through the establishment of professional positions, such as aquatic and air resource specialists, that assist multiple parks with natural resource management issues at a local level.

Network Programs

The complexity of the natural resource issues facing parks today necessitates communication and cooperation among all levels of the National Park Service and beyond. Four Challenge-initiated programs—Cooperative Ecosystem Studies Units, Exotic Plant Management Teams, Inventory and Monitoring Networks, and Research Learning Centers—facilitate this coordination. These programs organize parks into biogeographic networks, allowing them to accomplish much more together than they could individually. The networks work closely with park, regional, and national natural resource programs; federal and state agencies; universities; nonprofit organizations; and other partners to accomplish shared resource protection goals.

Cooperative Ecosystem Studies Units

Cooperative Ecosystem Studies Units (CESUs) are multi-agency partnerships with the nation's universities and other institutions. Participation in the CESUs enables the National Park Service to obtain high-quality science, usable knowledge for resource managers, responsive technical assistance, continuing education, and cost-effective research programs. The broad scope of CESUs includes the biological, physical, social, and cultural sciences needed to address natural and cultural resource management issues at multiple scales and in an ecosystem context.

Seventeen CESUs are based at host universities across the country and include partner colleges and universities, federal and state agencies, and private research and educational organizations. In FY 2011 the National Park Service supported research coordinators at 15 CESUs; two coordinators support two CESUs. Two additional positions—an archeologist and a historian—are located at two CESUs in the Intermountain Region, and a national coordinator is located in Washington, D.C. The NPS coordinators are "brokers," working with park and program managers to identify research, technical assistance, and education needs and to seek out and match specialized expertise and assistance available from the universities and federal partners.

Measuring a Texas tortoise at Palo Alto Battlefield National Historical Park, Texas
NPS/ROBERT WOODMAN

Heading out in the field for a study of ice patches as sources of archeological and paleoecological data, Glacier National Park, Montana
PHOTO COURTESY OF CRAIG LEE, UNIVERSITY OF COLORADO BOULDER

In FY 2011 CESUs facilitated 785 projects totaling more than $43 million (Table 2-1), representing a decrease of about 5 percent in both number of projects and dollars processed compared to FY 2010. The median number of partners was unchanged at 24, ranging from 13 to 47. Since FY 2001 the CESU network has initiated 7,243 projects totaling $358 million (Table 2-2) and provided unparalleled science and education support to the National Park Service.

In FY 2011 two CESUs completed five-year renewals with their host institutions: Chesapeake Watershed, hosted by Frostburg State University in Maryland, and Great Basin, hosted by University of Nevada, Reno. Research coordinators continued their involvement with other national natural resource programs, initiatives that cut across the NPS directorates, and interagency collaborations. Examples include participating in the NPS/National Geographic Society BioBlitz at Saguaro National Park (AZ), serving on technical committees and boards of directors for inventory and monitoring networks, and managing projects for the multi-agency Great Lakes Restoration Initiative.

The CESUs were actively involved in responding to climate change in FY 2011, including facilitating diverse projects related to climate change science, adaptation, mitigation, and communication. Research coordinators participated directly in climate change–related activities, including leading a multi-park vegetation phenology monitoring project, sponsoring and presenting at an annual regional climate science conference, and serving on the science working group of the NPS Climate Change Steering Committee.

CESU projects addressed many of the themes and objectives of the NPS *Call to Action*. Several projects are detailed later in this report, including development of a podcast series for Timpanogos Cave National Monument, Utah (ACTION 17: GO DIGITAL) and the *Bear Valley Visitor Center Lighting Retrofit Guide* for Point Reyes National Seashore, California (ACTION 23: GO GREEN), and participation in BioBlitzes at Saguaro National Park, Arizona, and George Washington Birthplace National Monument, Virginia (ACTION 7: NEXT GENERATION STEWARDS).

Table 2-1. Number of projects, partners, and agreements funding by region and individual Cooperative Ecosystem Studies Unit (CESU), FY 2011

		Total partners, projects, and funding from all sources, FY 2011		
Region	CESU	Partners [a]	Projects	Funding ($)
Alaska	North and West Alaska	13	52	3,030,577
Intermountain	Colorado Plateau	24	129	4,360,880
	Desert Southwest	24	47	1,509,331
	Rocky Mountains	22	157	10,723,710
Midwest	Great Plains	26	9	236,435
	Great Lakes-Northern Forest	47	29	1,826,995
	Great Rivers	27	14	676,705
National Capital	Chesapeake Watershed	22	34	1,884,980
Northeast	North Atlantic Coast	22	22	1,319,686
Pacific West	Californian	34	31	2,722,992
	Great Basin	22	24	1,489,387
	Hawaii-Pacific Islands	18	21	1,250,124
	Pacific Northwest	28	77	4,649,612
Southeast	Gulf Coast	41	55	1,179,364
	Piedmont-South Atlantic Coast	32	25	1,553,953
	South Florida/Caribbean	23	28	3,550,000
	Southern Appalachian Mountains	24	31	1,591,366
TOTAL			785	$43,556,097

[a] Because some agencies partner with more than one CESU, the total would equal more than the total listed in the text.

Cutting invasive tamarisk in Grand Canyon-Parashant National Monument, Arizona
NPS PHOTO

Table 2-2. Cooperative Ecosystems Studies Unit (CESU) projects and funding, FY 2001–FY 2011

Fiscal year	CESUs in network	Projects initiated	Total funding ($)
2001	8	260	10 million
2002	12	380	15 million
2003	16	540	19 million
2004	17	650	27 million
2005	17	635	32 million
2006	17	728	39 million
2007	17	848	43 million
2008	17	777	45 million
2009	17	804	38 million
2010	17	836	46 million
2011	17	785	44 million
TOTAL		7,243	$358 million

Exotic Plant Management Teams

Native communities of plants and animals and historical landscapes across the National Park System are threatened by invasive plant species. Exotic Plant Management Teams (EPMTs) were established to respond to this expanding problem. They contribute to invasive plant control goals servicewide by working closely with other NPS programs and cooperating with other federal agencies, tribal nations, state parks, and private landowners. This highly successful and collaborative effort increases the areas under invasive plant management and supports a landscape approach to invasive species management.

EPMTs participate in all aspects of invasive plant management including risk assessment, mapping, prevention, inventory, monitoring, treatment, and maintenance. Sixteen teams serve more than 225 parks across the country, providing guidance for all parks facing invasive plant issues and serving as first-line responders to exotic plant invasions. The teams are headquartered in a region or park and operate over a wide geographic area. Staffed by highly trained individuals with expertise in plant identification, plant ecology, invasive plant management, and pesticide use, the teams have emerged as local and regional invasive plant experts.

In FY 2011 EPMTs inventoried 2,127,588 acres within park boundaries. Teams monitored 18,373 acres and located 8,786 newly infested acres, which will be prioritized for treatment in future efforts. The teams treated more than 270 separate invasive species for a total of 7,848 acres. Combined, these activities represent the teams' role in the full range of invasive plant management from early detection through monitoring of program priorities and ultimately restoration of park vegetation to native-dominated communities.

A review of the EPMT program was completed in FY 2011 to reflect on activities since the program's inception in 2000, plan for challenges in the future, and improve processes and procedures to ensure long-term relevancy and short-term efficiencies. The review consisted of a survey, interviews, and on-site visits by NPS and non-NPS panel members. The program was cited for its excellent safety record. The review affirmed that the investment in the program has resulted in large gains in invasive plant management in parks. The review offered a number of recommendations, including developing a long-term strategic plan, establishing a servicewide advisory group, reviewing each EPMT's business model, and streamlining administrative procedures. National EPMT staff, along with regional and park staff, will continue to evaluate other models for invasive plant management to improve efficiency and effectiveness throughout the National Park System while implementing the review's high-priority recommendations.

Inventory and Monitoring Networks

The Inventory and Monitoring (I&M) Program is an essential part of the National Park Service's effort to revitalize the natural resource program and to improve park management through greater reliance on scientific

Sampling macroinvertebrates in Fredericksburg & Spotsylvania National Military Park, Virginia
NPS/STEPHIE BURKART

information. Thirty-two bioregional networks that share core funding, professional staff, and monitoring crews provide expertise and information to support 270 parks with significant natural resources. By leveraging limited funding and staff through partnerships and linking to park operations, the I&M networks provide scientifically sound, organized, and retrievable information about parks' natural resources to support management decision making, park planning, research, education, and public understanding. For most parks, the I&M Program provides the primary means of measuring the status and trends in the condition of park resources.

The I&M Program provides funding, technical assistance, and coordination for parks to complete 12 basic natural resource inventories and to monitor the condition, or "health," of park natural resources based on key vital signs. The basic natural resource inventories assess and document the current condition and knowledge of natural resources in parks and establish a solid baseline for long-term monitoring plans (CALL TO ACTION ITEM 28: PARK PULSE). The investigations increase our knowledge and understanding of park resources, including many new and exciting insights, and provide information to address a wide variety of resource management issues and activities. In FY 2011 the I&M Program completed an additional 42 inventory data sets for a total of 2,587 data sets (93.5 percent of all proposed data sets) developed and delivered to parks (Table 2-3). At current funding levels, the delivery of all 2,767 data sets to the 270 I&M parks will be completed in about five years.

Vital signs monitoring tracks a subset of physical, chemical, and biological elements and processes of park ecosystems that are selected to represent the overall health or condition of park resources, known or hypothesized effects of stressors, or elements that have important human values. As of September 2011, 100 percent of the 270 I&M parks had identified their vital signs, developed a state-of-the-art monitoring plan, and implemented operational monitoring of priority resources. All 270 I&M parks can now provide "current condition" estimates for key measurements of the condition of high-priority natural resources (Table 2-4). While funding limits monitoring to the highest priority vital signs or those where data are available from other sources, parks can expand monitoring efforts by augmenting Challenge funds with operational support, personnel, and funding from other sources; establishing partnerships; and monitoring several vital signs and parameters together. The number of networks and parks that expect to monitor a vital sign in various categories with currently available funding is summarized in Table 2-5.

During FY 2011 the I&M Program completed the integration of what used to be five separate, stand-alone data applications into the Integrated Resource Management Applications (IRMA) data system. The IRMA data system, which is based on Department of the Interior (DOI) and industry standards and best practices, is used to manage and deliver natural and cultural resource documents and datasets and will allow data exchange and integration among different data systems within and external to DOI agencies.

Inventory and monitoring results are used in each park's natural resource condition assessment, resource stewardship strategy, state of the park report, and other park planning documents (Table 2-4). Results are also provided to managers, planners, interpreters, scientists, and the general public. Combined with an effective education program, inventory and monitoring results can contribute to resolving not only park issues but also to larger quality-of-life issues that affect surrounding communities and can contribute significantly to the environmental health of the nation. As a direct result of the Challenge, the I&M Program has become a significant component of the overall scientific and information management infrastructure and expertise of the National Park Service.

Table 2-3. Number of Inventory and Monitoring Program parks out of the total 270 parks in the program that received the minimal set of inventory products identified in 1992 during FY 2001–FY 2011

Inventory	Fiscal year										
	2001	2002	2003	2004	2005	2006	2007	2008	2009	2010	2011
Natural resource bibliography	257	263	270	270	270	270	270	270	270	270	270
Base cartography data	248	260	270	270	270	270	270	270	270	270	270
Air quality data	250	250	250	270	270	270	270	270	270	270	270
Air quality related values	0	0	0	48	100	150	175	210	240	270	270
Climate inventory	0	197	270	270	270	270	270	270	270	270	270
Geologic resources inventory	2	14	17	52	68	92	117	138	164	184	204
Soil resources inventory	37	57	57	59	70	100	141	171	190	207	218
Water body classification	0	220	270	270	270	270	270	270	270	270	270
Baseline water quality data	225	270	270	270	270	270	270	270	270	270	270
Vegetation inventory	22	27	36	51	62	80	127	155	173	197	208
Species lists	210	270	270	270	270	270	270	270	270	270	270
Species status/distribution	0	0	0	3	44	100	200	270	270	270	270
TOTAL	1,251	1,828	1,982	2,103	2,234	2,412	2,650	2,834	2,927	3,018	3,060
Completed before 2001	473	473	473	473	473	473	473	473	473	473	473
GPRA actual	778	1,355	1,509	1,630	1,761	1,939	2,177	2,361	2,455	2,545	2,587
GPRA target	768	1,121	1,498	1,637	1,771	1,942	2,145	2,338	2,450	2,500	2,550
Percent GPRA complete[a]			54.5	58.9	63.6	70.1	78.7	85.3	88.7	92.0	93.5

[a]Percent GPRA complete values are based on the baseline of 2,767 total data sets to be delivered to the 270 I&M parks during the initial phase of natural resource inventory development.

Table 2-4. Annual accomplishments of the 270 Inventory and Monitoring Program parks in completing the planning and design of their long-term monitoring programs and implementing operational monitoring of vital signs, FY 2006–FY 2011, and projected completion, FY 2012–FY 2013. Data and expertise provided by the I&M networks are a key source of data for park natural resource condition assessments, resource stewardship strategies, and other park planning and management efforts and are now being used to help develop state of the park reports that summarize status and trends in resource condition for selected parks.

Actual and projected accomplishments for vital signs monitoring and resource assessments		Number of parks completed by end of fiscal year						Number of parks projected	
		2006	2007	2008	2009	2010	2011	2012	2013
Planning and design phase	Identify and synthesize existing information	270	270	270	270	270	270	270	270
	Prioritize and select vital signs	250	270	270	270	270	270	270	270
	Monitoring plan completed, peer-reviewed, and approved—operational monitoring begun	157	197	253	270	270	270	270	270
	"Current condition" values available for specific vital signs—operational monitoring ongoing	104	157	197	253	253	270	270	270
Monitoring and assessments completed	Park natural resource condition assessments completed	0	0	1	8	13	32	52	72
	Park resource stewardship strategy plans completed that incorporate results from vital signs monitoring and natural resource condition assessments	0	1	1	3	5	15	18	20

Setting traps for amphibian and reptile sampling in Gulf Islands National Seashore, Florida
NPS/ROBERT WOODMAN

Table 2-5. Number of parks in the Inventory and Monitoring Program that will monitor each vital sign category using existing funding (including funding from partnerships where the networks will deliver data summaries to park managers and planners). Vital signs that will be monitored in fewer than 29 parks are not listed.

Vital sign category	Example measures (varies by network)	Number of parks
Weather and climate	Temperature, precipitation, wind speed, ice on/off	246
Water chemistry	pH, temperature, dissolved oxygen, conductivity	207
Land cover and use	Area in each land cover and use type; patch size and pattern	204
Invasive/exotic plants	Early detection, presence/absence, area	203
Birds	Species composition, distribution, abundance	192
Surface water dynamics	Discharge/flow rates (cfs), gauge/stage height, lake elevation, spring/seep volume, sea-level rise	149
Ozone	Ozone concentration, damage to sensitive vegetation	141
Wet and dry deposition	Wet deposition chemistry, sulfur dioxide concentrations	114
Visibility and particulate matter	IMPROVE network; visibility and fine particles	113
Vegetation complexes	Plant community diversity, relative species/guild abundance, structure/age class, incidence of disease	103
Mammals	Species composition, distribution, abundance	95
Forest/woodland communities	Community diversity, coverage and abundance, condition and vigor classes, regeneration	95
Soil function and dynamics	Soil nutrients, cover and composition of biological soil crust communities, soil aggregate stability	94
Aquatic macroinvertebrates	Species composition and abundance	92
Fire and fuel dynamics	Long-term trend of fire frequency, average fire size, average burn severity, total area affected by fire	90
Stream/river channel characteristics	Channel width, depth, and gradient, sinuosity, channel cross-section, pool frequency and depth, particle size	88
Threatened and endangered species and communities	Population estimates, distribution, sex and age ratios	85
Air contaminants	Concentrations of SOCs, PCBs, DDT, Hg	75
Groundwater dynamics	Flow rate, depth to ground water, withdrawal rates, recharge rates, volume in aquifer	69
Amphibians and reptiles	Species distribution and abundance, population age/size structure, species diversity, percent area occupied	54
Insect pests	Extent of insect-related mortality, distribution and extent of standing dead/stressed/diseased trees, early detection	53
Wetland communities	Species composition and percent cover, distribution and density of selected plants, canopy height, aerial extent	51
Grassland/herb communities	Composition, structure, abundance, changes in treeline	51
Fishes	Community composition, abundance, distribution, age classes, occupancy, invasive species	49
Nutrient dynamics	Nitrate, ammonia, DON, nitrite, orthophosphate, total K	45
Primary production	Normalized differential vegetation index (NDVI), change in length of growing season, carbon fixation	41
Riparian communities	Species composition and percent cover, distribution and density of selected plants, canopy height	38
Microorganisms	Fecal coliform, E. coli, cyanobacteria	30
Water toxics	Organic and inorganic toxics, heavy metals	30
Invasive/exotic animals	Invasive species present, distribution, vegetation types invaded, early detection at invasion points	29
Coastal/oceanographic features and processes	Rate of shoreline change, sea surface elevations, area and degree of subsidence through relative elevation data	29

Undergraduate student and local high school teacher preparing a soil core collected at Indiana Dunes National Lakeshore, Indiana, for a vegetation history
NPS/JOY MARBURGER

Research Learning Centers

Research Learning Centers (RLCs) support and integrate scientific research, education, and communication in the national parks. They accomplish this by working with hundreds of local and national partners to facilitate research projects in the parks, communicate research results to park managers and other audiences, develop innovative science education programs and products, and conduct a wide range of public outreach activities that help increase science literacy.

Twelve RLCs were established with initial funding from the Challenge beginning in FY 2001. An additional seven RLCs are funded by partners and existing park base funds. Each RLC serves a park or a local network of parks and is staffed by professionals with expertise in natural resource science and education.

The RLCs are highly effective at meeting the diverse long-standing and emerging needs of the parks. Because they combine research, education, communication, and partnerships, the RLCs are ideal for increasing and disseminating knowledge about issues such as climate change impacts on park resources, development and land use surrounding parks, loss of cultural heritage, and other large-scale and multi-dimensional threats. Similarly, by making scientific inquiry a part of the visitor experience, the RLCs increase the relevance of parks to the American public.

In FY 2011 the RLCs continued to support a wide range of research projects. For example, the Appalachian Highlands Science Learning Center permitted or facilitated 245 projects, ranging from the comparative physiology of stream insects to models of soil recovery from acid deposition. Those projects included scientists from 72 universities, 11 public agencies, and 21 other organizations. Most RLCs provided low-cost accommodations to researchers, typically in the range of 1,000–2,000 person-nights. Collectively RLC support for past research yielded more than 200 scientific publications in FY 2011, more than half of which were peer-reviewed journal articles. See Table 2-6 (page 10) for a summary of RLC activities in FY 2011.

The RLCs adopted many creative and effective means of communicating scientific information to diverse audiences in FY 2011. Conferences, research symposia, and science seminars (e.g., the eighth annual Waterton-Glacier Science and History Conference organized by the Crown of the Continent RLC) remained popular, typically attracting hundreds of resource managers, academic scientists, students, and the general public. Publications included Gateway RLC's biweekly "Field Notes" newsletter summarizing field activities and research results for park staff and visitors. Online products included regular public webinars about scientific issues (e.g., the marine science series developed in part by the Ocean Alaska Science and Learning Center); an interactive website for teachers' professional development (Greater Yellowstone Science Learning Center); and a live broadcast from eight culturally significant parks to participants in a DOI Diversity Days event in Washington, D.C. (Southern California RLC).

The RLCs also supported the NPS *Call to Action*. Examples of FY 2011 projects included a podcast about ocean acidification by the Pacific Coast Science and Learning Center (ACTION 17: GO DIGITAL); the use of "Picture Posts" by the Urban Ecology Research Learning Alliance to enable urbanites to monitor environmental change in Washington, D.C., parks (ACTION 7: NEXT GENERATION STEWARDS); and the provision of graduate research fellowships in northern Alaskan parks by Murie Science and Learning Center (ACTION 20: SCHOLARLY PURSUITS).

Students measuring groundwater quality at Junior Ranger Ecology Camp, Congaree National Park, South Carolina
NPS/THERESA THOM

Table 2-6. Research Learning Center activities, FY 2011

Activity	Value
Research projects supported	861
Housing for researchers	
Person-nights	13,999
Savings to researchers	$858,194
Publications stemming from research and education projects	
Peer-reviewed scientific papers	173
Other publications	127
Students involved in research and education projects	
Graduate students	222
Undergraduate students	390
Interns and volunteers (including high school students)	1,548
Partnerships	
Colleges and universities	220
K–12 formal and informal education organizations	239
Other	304

Webcam view of Halema'uma'u Crater, Hawaii Volcanoes National Park, Hawaii
NPS PHOTO

Servicewide Natural Resource Programs

Servicewide natural resource programs provide much-needed services to the nearly 400 units of the National Park Service. Within each discipline, program staff offer policy and regulatory expertise, provide technical assistance and advice, help develop plans and proposals, and guide education and outreach efforts. Eight servicewide programs provide leadership in specialized areas:

- Air Quality
- Biological Resource Management
- Climate Change Response
- Environmental Quality
- Geologic Resources
- Natural Sounds and Night Skies
- Social Science
- Water Resources

Challenge funding enhanced the Air Quality, Biological Resource Management, Geologic Resources, and Water Resources programs. FY 2011 servicewide natural resource program funding is included in Appendix B.

Air Quality

The Air Quality program is responsible for preserving, protecting, and enhancing air quality and air quality–related values in the national parks. The program engages in regulatory and policy arenas, interpretation and outreach, air quality monitoring, and research and analysis to accomplish this goal.

The program routinely works with states, the U.S. Environmental Protection Agency (EPA), and other agencies and stakeholders to develop air policies and strategies that protect park resources. In FY 2011 regulatory and policy collaborations included working with the U.S. Forest Service (USFS) and the U.S. Fish and Wildlife Service (USFWS) to review 14 state and two federal regional haze plans. These plans will result in major reductions in visibility-impairing pollutants in parks and other protected areas. Program staff reviewed 12 new source permit applications for projects proposing to locate near NPS-managed areas, including independent air quality impact and control technology assessments. In cooperation with the USFS and USFWS, the program published the *Federal Land Managers' Interagency Guidance for Nitrogen and Sulfur Deposition Analyses* to provide air regulators, permit applicants, and other project proponents with EPA methods and information for assessing impacts of air pollutants on NPS resources. Additionally, program staff worked with USFS, USFWS, EPA, and the Bureau of Land Management (BLM) to craft and finalize a memorandum of understanding to work cooperatively in dealing with environmental compliance documents and mitigation related to oil and gas development activities on federal lands.

Interpretation and outreach efforts include synthesizing air quality data and analyses, interpreting and disseminating air quality information for educational and other public purposes, and facilitating air quality–related interpretive projects and activities in parks. In FY 2011 the Air Quality Web Camera (Webcam) Network, consisting of 19 digital cameras at 18 parks, had more than 7 million "visits." New digital cameras were installed at **Hawaii Volcanoes National Park (HI)** and **Shenandoah National Park (VA)**, addressing CALL TO ACTION ITEM 17: GO DIGITAL. Program staff also assisted several national parks (**Acadia [ME]; Great Smoky Mountains [NC, TN]; Mammoth Cave [KY]; Rocky Mountain [CO]; Sequoia and Kings Canyon [CA]; Shenandoah [VA];** and **Yosemite [CA]**) with their ozone and fine particle health advisory programs to alert park visitors and employees when concentrations have the potential to reach unhealthy levels.

Monitoring and research activities identify status and trends of air quality conditions in NPS units; provide air quality assessments; produce data for special studies and other research; and enhance our understanding of the specific causes of air pollution, the reaction of pollutants in the atmosphere, pollutant deposition pathways, and visibility degradation (CALL TO ACTION ITEM 28: PARK PULSE). In collaboration with several organizations and agencies, the program operates at least five monitoring networks in parks measuring more than 10 parameters including ambient gases, meteorology, deposition chemistry, particulate matter, and visibility. In FY 2011 accomplishments included measuring ozone with portable systems in 16 parks as part of the I&M Program; new ammonia monitoring in 14 parks; a new monitoring station at **Grand Teton National Park (WY)** to measure ozone,

Extracting fish tissue for analysis of contaminant effects at Great Sand Dunes National Park and Preserve, Colorado
NPS PHOTO

Biodiversity youth ambassador at the closing ceremony at the 2011 BioBlitz at Saguaro National Park, Arizona
NPS/TODD M. EDGAR

wet deposition, and optical visibility and a webcam; and a sulfur dioxide sensor network at seven locations around **Hawaii Volcanoes National Park (HI)**, as well as a particulate monitor to provide warning of unhealthy air conditions to the park and the public.

Through its ecological effects work, the program has identified natural resources sensitive to air pollutants in more than 200 parks, as well as specific ecosystem indicators that respond to pollution and the thresholds associated with a given response. This information helps to protect park resources by establishing park management goals and reporting and communicating on resource trends and condition (CALL TO ACTION ITEM 28: PARK PULSE). In FY 2011 program staff cooperated with Oregon State University to assess contaminant levels in 53 fish from five national parks (**Great Sand Dunes [CO] and Wrangell-St. Elias [AK] national parks and preserves and Lassen Volcanic [CA], Rocky Mountain [CO], and Yosemite [CA] national parks**). The pesticides DDE and dieldrin were found in fish in some study lakes (as a result of atmospheric deposition) at concentrations above human health consumption thresholds. Staff also facilitated several projects to estimate the amount of atmospherically derived pollutants (critical loads) that lakes, streams, and forest soils in the northeast and southeast United States can sustain indefinitely without damage.

Biological Resource Management

The Biological Resource Management program provides leadership in the conservation, preservation, restoration, and stewardship of biological resources for the National Park Service. Staff provide professional, science-based support to manage and protect biological resources and related ecosystem processes in the National Park System. The program focuses its efforts in five branches of technical expertise:

The Development and New Initiatives Branch provides targeted partnership and philanthropy development and technical assistance on fundraising, agreements, and volunteer activities to benefit natural resource management in parks and regions. Highlights from FY 2011 included the signing of the Project-WET and NPS Partnership Agreement, which supports the creation of the $3.2 million "Discover the Waters of the National Parks" project to promote place-based, standards-based education on NPS water resources (CALL TO ACTION ITEM 16: LIVE AND LEARN). This partnership was a highlight of a global water conference, Sustaining the Blue Planet, in September 2011, and participants from 40 different countries spontaneously donated to the Discover the Waters project.

The Human Dimensions of Biological Resources Branch addresses the critical interface between the human and ecological components of biological resource management. Staff work to better understand the impacts of biological resources and associated management actions on the public and the impacts from the public on biological resources and management in parks. Focus areas include human dimensions to improve understanding of visitor and stakeholder perceptions; tools and consistent messaging to address habituation in wildlife; integrated pest management to reduce risks from pests and pest-related management activities particularly in structures within parks; and biodiversity discovery/citizen science to engage citizens and scientists in discovering, cataloging, and learning more about life in parks. Highlights from FY 2011 included co-developing workshops integrating social science into climate change response planning in protected areas; serving on the Mexican Wolf Recovery Team and The Wildlife Society Blue Ribbon Panel on the Future of the Wildlife Profession; reviewing nearly 3,000 pesticide use proposals; and assisting with coordination, outreach, and evaluation for NPS BioBlitzes and All-Taxa Biodiversity Inventories (CALL TO ACTION ITEM 7: NEXT GENERATION STEWARDS).

The Restoration and Adaptation Branch addresses servicewide needs in restoration science and technology and emerging questions and solutions for adapting to globally changing environments. Efforts emphasized collaboration across jurisdictions to manage resource issues at appropriate scales. Staff provided leadership through interagency efforts and the network of EPMTs to address invasive species, such as Miconia in Hawaii and tamarisk across the western United States. In FY 2011 staff signed a memorandum of understanding with the American Chestnut Foundation to research, monitor, and implement pilot

High school students collecting burs from a chinquapin tree, a relative of the chestnut, for a restoration project in Buffalo National River, Arkansas
NPS PHOTO

projects within parks to conserve the American chestnut; collaborated with interagency staff on United States–Mexico border infrastructure and environment issues; and helped develop the *DOI Adaptive Management Applications Guide* and the *National Fish, Wildlife, and Plants Climate Adaptation Strategy*.

The Wildlife Conservation Branch provides leadership to collaboratively address complex wildlife conservation issues and to provide strategic policy guidance regarding conservation of resources and related ecosystem processes that affect wildlife and their habitats in national parks. Staff coordinate servicewide wildlife management efforts to ensure policy interpretation, compliance, and consistency and that management efforts are technically adequate and scientifically credible and robust. They serve as technical advisors for activities relating to servicewide management of wildlife and wildlife habitats. FY 2011 accomplishments included initiating and leading the first comprehensive review of ungulate management in NPS history; developing long-term guidance for enhanced bison conservation (CALL TO ACTION ITEM 26: BACK HOME ON THE RANGE); providing technical support to federal and state agencies on amphibian and reptile conservation through the Partnership for Amphibians and Reptiles; expanding the NPS Migration Conservation Initiative by incorporating national and international colleagues and strategies (CALL TO ACTION ITEM 22: SCALING UP); and collaborating on a new NPS strategy to effectively conserve and restore threatened, endangered, and at-risk species.

The Wildlife Health Branch provides professional veterinary assistance and consultation to parks and regions to minimize negative impacts of introduced diseases on wildlife. Staff serve as agency leaders in developing national guidance and plans for managing emerging diseases such as white-nose syndrome of bats and chronic wasting disease of deer and elk. Through close collaboration between the Wildlife Health Branch and the NPS Office of Public Health, the National Park Service has implemented a One Health approach, which recognizes that human and animal health are inextricably linked, to improve the health of all species and the environment (CALL TO ACTION ITEM 6: TAKE A HIKE, CALL ME IN THE MORNING). In FY 2011 staff developed a managers' guide for addressing plague, published collaborative research aimed at improving effective communication on disease risk from wildlife, and investigated the benefits that healthy wildlife contribute to human health. In addition to addressing wildlife disease issues, staff work to improve the health and welfare of wildlife by providing onsite assistance and project review on issues such as fertility control, field anesthesia, and humane handling and use of animals in parks.

Biological Resource Management competitive funds are used to address resource management issues concerning ecosystems, ecosystem processes, wildlife, and vegetation throughout the National Park System. In FY 2011, 11 projects totaling $246,000 focused on natural resource issues such as determining the effects of beach activities on shorebirds, protecting rare bat colonies and imperiled plants, and assessing factors affecting fish diversity and abundance (Appendix C).

Climate Change Response

The Climate Change Response Program fosters communication, provides scientific information and planning guidance, and supports adaptation and mitigation actions to protect natural and cultural resources in the face of climate change. It is a distributed program with staff in several national natural resource programs (Geologic Resources, Biological Resource Management, and Water Resources) as well as the Cultural Resource Stewardship and Science Directorate and four regional offices (Northeast, Southeast, Pacific West, and Intermountain). Expertise includes climate change science and modeling, interpretation and education, resource management, landscape connectivity, monitoring, planning, coastal hazards, cultural anthropology, and renewable and efficient energy use. The NPS *Climate Change Response Strategy*, released in September 2010, describes goals and objectives to guide NPS actions through four integrated components: science, adaptation, mitigation, and communication. In FY 2011 staff realized a number of accomplishments designed to fulfill the goals of the strategy:

- Authored more than 30 peer-reviewed publications and technical reports and gave more than 50 presentations on climate change for managers, resource profession-

Desert bighorn sheep
NPS PHOTO

Talking points document for Atlantic Coast bioregion
NPS PHOTO

als, interpreters, park rangers, scientists, non-governmental organizations, policy and decision makers, and the public.

- Finalized detailed work plans and began enhanced monitoring for 94 parks in 13 I&M networks to document changing conditions in vulnerable parks. CALL TO ACTION ITEM 28: PARK PULSE
- Completed two vulnerability assessments at **Point Reyes National Seashore (CA)** and **Puʻukoholā Heiau National Historic Site/Kaloko-Honokōhau National Historical Park (HI)**. CALL TO ACTION ITEM 28: PARK PULSE
- Initiated two new assessments on climate refugia and connectivity for desert bighorn sheep and four species of concern in southwestern Utah parks and monuments.
- Trained more than 150 people in seven areas on the use of climate change scenarios in long-range planning.
- Initiated $2.7 million in applied research projects in parks (Appendix D).
- Coordinated with university and non-governmental organizational partners on five workshops, 16 sites visits, and a series of surveys with park staff and visitors to explore climate change interpretation and education needs and activities in parks.
- Completed 11 bioregional "talking points" documents for messaging climate change impacts on parks.
- Developed and implemented an interpretive training module on science literacy and climate change for front-line interpreters. CALL TO ACTION ITEM 30: TOOLS OF THE TRADE
- Placed 14 interns and 11 fellows in parks and offices across the country through the George Melendez Wright Internship and Fellowship programs. CALL TO ACTION ITEM 20: SCHOLARLY PURSUITS
- Connected to DOI Climate Science Center and Landscape Conservation Cooperative networks contributing to science needs assessments and enhanced regional capacity through placement of three adaptation coordinators in the Pacific Islands, South Atlantic, and North Atlantic Landscape Conservation Cooperatives. CALL TO ACTION ITEM 22: SCALING UP

Environmental Quality

This program serves a key role in ensuring that the National Park Service meets the requirements of the 1916 Organic Act and makes informed decisions that maintain the unspoiled beauty, rich landscapes, and abundant resources of our parks. The Environmental Quality program helps the National Park Service accomplish its mission through environmental planning and compliance, resource protection, and external review. Many of the projects under these areas are multi-year efforts that involve other agencies at the federal and state levels. In FY 2011 the Environmental Quality program merged with the Social Science program (see entry on page 17).

Environmental Planning and Compliance Branch staff provide policy development, technical assistance, training, and project management to parks in the areas of impact analysis and conservation planning under the National Environmental Policy Act (NEPA) and related statutes. Staff assist parks with complex, controversial, and potentially precedent-setting NEPA analyses and decisions and provide assistance that may not be available at the park or regional levels. In FY 2011 technical staff managed environmental planning projects in 20 parks, including **Yellowstone National Park (ID, MT, WY)** winter use planning; environmental assessment to evaluate alternatives for revitalizing **Jefferson National Expansion Memorial (MO)**; off-road vehicle management plans for **Cape Hatteras National Seashore (NC), Cape Lookout National Seashore (NC), Lake Meredith National Recreation Area (TX),** and **Glen Canyon National Recreation Area (AZ, UT); Sequoia and Kings Canyon National Parks (CA)** wilderness stewardship plan; **Rock Creek Park (DC)** white-tailed deer management plan; and **Golden Gate National Recreation Area (CA)** dog management plan.

Resource Protection Branch staff provide technical assistance, training, case management, and restoration project management to help parks address incident-caused injuries to park resources. Under the Park System Resource Protection Act (PSRPA, 16 U.S.C. 19jj); Oil Pollution Act (OPA, 33 U.S.C. 2701, et seq.); and Comprehensive Environmental Response, Compensation, and Liability Act (CERCLA, 42 U.S.C. 9601, et seq.), the National Park Service is authorized to take actions to prevent or minimize injuries to park resources, assess and seek recovery of

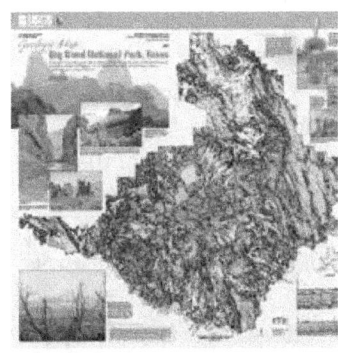

Geologic map for Big Bend National Park, Texas
NPS PHOTO

Preparing a well in Big South Fork National River and Recreation Area, Tennessee, for permanent plugging and abandonment
NPS PHOTO

compensatory damages, and restore injured resources associated with discharges of oil, releases of hazardous substances, and other incidents. In FY 2011 the program facilitated cost documentation and reimbursement efforts for the Deepwater Horizon Oil Spill response and led servicewide efforts for damage assessment and early restoration. Staff managed 64 PSRPA cases, three OPA cases, and four CERCLA cases, yielding 39 settlements. During FY 2011 recovered funds deposited in DOI's Natural Resource Damage Assessment and Restoration Fund totaled $1.74 million; funds withdrawn for restoration totaled $1.72 million.

Geologic Resources

The Geologic Resources program provides scientific, policy, and technical leadership and guidance to NPS resource managers, stakeholders, and decision makers for the protection and management of geologic and interdependent ecosystem resources of the National Park System. The program carries out an array of activities in six broad categories:

Geologic features, landscapes, and processes staff provide parks with technical assistance related to paleontological resources, cave and karst resources, coastal geology, geologic mapping, soil resources, and active geological processes. Staff helped develop cave and karst management plans, reviewed cave and karst resource protection programs, and led the federal partnership with the National Cave and Karst Research Institute. The opening of the new building in Carlsbad, New Mexico, to house the institute was a landmark event in 2011. In addition, the institute conducted research at **White Sands National Monument (NM)** supporting a characterization of local and sub-regional groundwater hydrology. Geologic Resources staff also led NPS involvement in developing DOI regulations governing the management and protection of paleontological resources on federal lands, as required by the Omnibus Public Lands Management Act of 2009. Staff coordinated National Fossil Day, which attracted more than 130 affiliated organizations and held dozens of events in more than 20 states, including a "kick-off" event on the National Mall in Washington, D.C. (CALL TO ACTION ITEM 16: LIVE AND LEARN). Additionally, staff completed digital geologic maps for 20 parks and geologic reports for 18 parks and worked with partners to complete soil resource inventories for 11 parks (CALL TO ACTION ITEM 28: PARK PULSE). Coastal geology staff assisted with hurricane and storm impacts, restoration, and coastal resource inventory and monitoring.

Energy and mineral development staff provide assistance in addressing energy and mineral development issues inside and adjacent to park boundaries through expertise in mining, petroleum geology, petroleum engineering, regulations, policy, reclamation, and impact mitigation. At present, 12 parks contain 668 nonfederal oil and gas operations, and 15 parks contain a total of 1,200 mining claims. During FY 2011 staff provided park-specific assistance on energy- and mineral-related issues to more than 25 parks in six regions and continued to revise NPS regulations governing the exercise of non-federal oil and gas rights in parks. In FY 2011 the program led efforts to address park protection concerns with conventional oil and gas, shale gas, and renewable energy projects outside park boundaries. Program input into overarching interagency efforts, such as regional planning documents, assisted more than 100 parks.

Restoration–disturbed lands and abandoned mineral lands staff prepare technical guidance, review park work plans for technical adequacy, and provide oversight for disturbed lands restoration projects in parks (CALL TO ACTION ITEM 22: SCALING UP). In FY 2011 the program initiated projects in nine parks, including three projects that restored approximately 9.1 acres and provided a focused plan to restore hundreds of additional acres of severely disturbed land in three unique western mountain park settings. Six additional projects are multi-year projects that will be completed in FY 2012 or 2013. Staff also provide oversight, coordination, and technical support on land restoration and human safety hazard mitigation at abandoned mineral land (AML) sites in parks (CALL TO ACTION ITEM 24: INVEST WISELY). In FY 2011 the program completed all hazardous feature closure and reclamation work under a $24.57 million appropriation from the American Recovery and Reinvestment Act of 2009 (ARRA), addressing hazardous or environmentally detrimental conditions at 910 AML features

Hurricane Irene damage at Cape Lookout National Seashore, North Carolina
NPS PHOTO

in 31 parks in 15 states. These projects addressed approximately 10 percent of the total estimated AML needs of the National Park Service.

Geologic resource information for park planning staff provide geosciences data and policy input to planning documents and nonfederal oil and gas planning efforts in parks and offer resource-specific technical assistance and data and technical reviews of park planning documents. In FY 2011 staff provided geoscience information and comments on specific projects, including an environmental impact statement for nonfederal oil and gas development at **Big South Fork National River and Recreation Area (KY, TN)**; general management plans at **Gulf Islands National Seashore (FL)**, **Fort Matanzas National Monument (FL)**, **Assateague Island National Seashore (MD, VA)**, **Cape Hatteras National Seashore (NC)**, and **Golden Gate National Recreation Area (CA)**; shoreline management plan at **Indiana Dunes National Lakeshore (IN)**; dredged material management plan at **Cape Lookout National Seashore (NC)**; long-range transportation plan at **Golden Gate National Recreation Area (CA)**; resource stewardship strategy at **Pecos National Historical Park (NM)**; and geologic resource impairment guidance for the Environmental Quality and Air Resources programs (CALL TO ACTION ITEM 28: PARK PULSE).

Climate change impacts and vulnerabilities staff help parks face the challenge of managing resources with respect to climate change (e.g., rates of shoreline erosion in parks are increasing as sea level rises, storms intensify, and storm surges reach farther inland). The *Storm Recovery Plan for Cape Lookout National Seashore* **(NC)** was signed in May 2011 and used to protect natural and cultural resources during the response to Hurricane Irene in August–September. Staff also worked with the U.S. Department of Agriculture (USDA) Natural Resources Conservation Service National Soil Survey Laboratory on a climate change and carbon sequestration project to use soil resources inventory data from several parks for the ongoing efforts of the National Rapid Soil Carbon Assessment Program to inventory soil carbon stocks on private, federal, and tribal lands.

Active geological processes and hazards staff help parks assess and evaluate active geological processes such as erosion, landslides, rock falls, and tsunamis and protect park visitors and infrastructure from the effects of these active processes. Staff participated in an All-Hazards Resource Advisor (READ) workshop to develop a web-based training course for training DOI natural and cultural resource professionals about the roles and responsibilities of a READ in emergency response. Staff helped the Vanishing Treasures Program and **Canyonlands National Park (UT)** to assess the stability and hazard potential of a highly visited archaeological site near Aztec Butte Arch. Also in FY 2011 staff provided incident-related technical assistance following Hurricane Irene at **Cape Lookout National Seashore (NC)** by providing policy and permitting assistance in responding to proposed actions that could impact processes in park coastal waters.

Natural Sounds and Night Skies

The Natural Sounds and Night Skies program protects, maintains, and restores soundscape and night sky resources and values by working in partnership with parks and others to increase scientific and public understanding of the value and character of these resources.

The Natural Sounds program works with the Federal Aviation Administration (FAA) to implement the National Parks Air Tour Management Act of 2000. Specifically, staff offer technical assistance to parks through monitoring acoustic conditions, collecting and analyzing data, developing ambient acoustic baseline information, and providing planning assistance including drafting and reviewing park plans and NEPA documents.

In FY 2011 the Natural Sounds program continued to expand both capacity and productivity by working with partners. Partnership projects included acoustic monitoring for air tour management plans with the FAA and Volpe National Transportation Systems Center, model validation and improvement with the Federal Interagency Committee on Aircraft Noise, park-based social science/visitor use research, and soundscape planning and workshops. Staff also collaborated with the Acoustical Society of America, American National Standards Committee,

Sound monitoring equipment in Denali National Park, Alaska
NPS/SHAN BURSON

USS *Arizona* Memorial, World War II Valor in the Pacific National Monument, Hawaii
NPS PHOTO

and International Standards Organization on developing consensus-based acoustical standards for protected areas.

In FY 2011 Natural Sounds staff performed acoustic monitoring at 24 units, completed 11 acoustic reports, and assisted 22 parks with military overflight issues. Staff developed prototype microphone systems that approach or exceed the human threshold of hearing at a cost that is more than ten times less expensive than commercially available products, developed an extremely precise acoustical time indicator based on GPS technology, and created a remote collaring device to continuously record the acoustical environments of wildlife near energy developments.

The Night Skies program was established in 1999 with the initial goal of developing instrumentation and methods to quantify night sky quality. Inventory of night sky quality in parks began shortly thereafter, and data have been collected at 96 parks to date. Staff now work on broader protection of natural lightscapes—the visual quality of a park's nighttime landscape that is dependent on natural light sources and darkness. This is accomplished by measuring current resource conditions, facilitating the science of lightscape management, reporting on existing conditions, encouraging the enjoyment and public understanding of the night, safeguarding nocturnal habitat, restoring views of starry skies through lighting retrofits, collaborating with gateway communities, and leading the agency and nation in lightscape stewardship (CALL TO ACTION ITEM 27: STARRY, STARRY NIGHT). The Night Skies program is on the leading edge of technological developments that will improve our ability to assess the portion of the measured "sky glow" that can be attributed to artificial light as opposed to the naturally occurring light from stars, the solar system, and Earth's atmosphere. Using state-of-the-art portable photometric equipment combined with rigorous data processing and calibration, these methods are recognized in the international scientific community for exceptional resolution and accuracy in the measurement of light pollution.

The data and images collected using tested and peer-reviewed methods provide a qualitative measure of sky brightness and its deviation from natural conditions. The maps and data help park managers convey to the public the ramifications of outdoor lighting practices, evoke a sense of awe and beauty, and frame the night sky as a resource and part of the park scenery. Staff are tracking new energy developments and developing best management practices for outdoor lighting that is both energy efficient and night sky friendly (CALL TO ACTION ITEM 23: GO GREEN).

In FY 2011 staff conducted night sky quality assessments at 19 parks and developed a method for subtracting natural light sources from data, enabling isolation of light pollution. They provided comments on and mitigation strategies for approximately 15 park planning documents and five external energy developments. Working with partners to protect the night sky, staff engaged in a cooperative agreement with the International Dark-Sky Association to assist in identifying common lighting solutions for parks and partnered with Clemson University on a social science survey of park managers' attitudes and activities addressing natural lightscapes. The Dark Sky Ambassador program was expanded to 14 parks, where volunteers contacted more than 43,000 visitors.

See Appendix E for a list of projects funded through the Natural Sounds fund source.

Social Science

The Social Science program conducts and facilitates research that provides public input into park planning and management, investigates economic interactions between parks and nearby communities, and develops methods and techniques to improve the management of visitor use. For example, the program conducted research to determine which type of ticket reservation system for the new visitor center at the USS *Arizona* Memorial at World War II Valor in the Pacific National Monument (HI) would maximize the public's opportunity to visit the memorial and adjacent attractions operated by park partners. Additional research is described below for continuing survey research projects such as the Visitor Services Project. Parks use this information to improve visitor services, encourage public engagement, protect natural and cultural resources, and manage resources more effectively.

U.S. Geological Survey staff checking a minnow trap in Iceberg Canyon in Glen Canyon National Recreation Area, Arizona and Utah
NPS/MELISSA TRAMMELL

Installing a water level sensor at Lake Lucero in White Sands National Monument, New Mexico
NPS/C. FILIPPONE

The Social Science program focuses on the following key functions:

The Comprehensive Survey of the American Public provides key insights into the knowledge, opinions, and behavior of both visitors and non-visitors regarding parks. In FY 2011 the National Park Service published the first of a series of reports resulting from this survey. Comparisons between the first comprehensive survey conducted in 2000 with the second comprehensive survey conducted in 2008–2009 provide relevant insights for park management. For example, in the 2000 survey one-third of survey respondents could name a valid NPS unit they had visited in the previous two years; in the 2008–2009 survey, that proportion increased to nearly one-half. In both surveys, the biggest perceived barriers to visitation included not knowing much about NPS units, the time required to get to one, and the costs of hotels and food.

The Money Generation Model estimates the economic impact of park visitation on surrounding communities and economies in terms of employment and sales. These quantifiable measures of the economic benefits of park visitation are used in planning, budgeting, marketing, and policy analysis. This model indicates that in 2010 park visitation supported 258,000 jobs nationwide and generated $31 billion in sales within the national economy, indicating that national parks are an economic engine for the United States.

The Public Use Statistics function establishes visitor counting protocols servicewide and provides visitation statistics and forecasts for parks and other units administered by the National Park Service. The *Statistical Abstract 2010* reports a total of 281 million recreation visits throughout the National Park System.

The Visitor Services Project conducts customized, park-specific studies of visitors—who they are, what they do, and what their opinions are. Park managers use these data to improve operations, protect resources, and better serve the public. In FY 2011 the Visitor Services Project conducted 16 studies in 11 parks.

The annual Visitor Survey Card measures visitor satisfaction at more than 328 units of the National Park System and gathers data concerning visitor understanding of a park's significance. It is the primary source of data used to measure the GPRA goals of visitor satisfaction (goal IIa1A) and visitor understanding (goal IIb1). During FY 2011 the overall level of visitor satisfaction was 97 percent, including 93 percent for park facilities, 95 percent for visitor services, and 95 percent for recreational opportunities.

Through technical assistance, Social Science staff work with parks, regions, and programs to obtain Office of Management and Budget approval for surveys of visitors and the public under the Paperwork Reduction Act. In FY 2011, 39 surveys were approved.

Water Resources

The Water Resources program provides leadership for the preservation, protection, and management of the water and aquatic resources in NPS units. Water resource issues include policy, planning, and regulatory review; water quality; water rights; floodplain management; erosion and sediment control; fisheries management; protection of wetland and riparian habitats; and ocean and coastal resources. In FY 2011 Water Resources staff managed four programs established by the Challenge—vital signs water quality monitoring, natural resource condition assessments, field-based aquatic resource management specialists, and water resource protection projects—as well as the Oceans and Coastal Resources program. Water resources projects are listed in Appendix F.

Fifteen field-based aquatic resource professionals received funding in 2011, which included filling a National Capital/Northeast Region shared position vacancy. These specialists provide park managers with locally based expertise to address high-priority aquatic resource needs. Location of these professionals within regions and at parks reduces transportation costs, provides rapid access for park needs, and allows these resource experts to become more familiar with local issues.

Natural resource condition assessments develop science-based information for park-level resource planning, decision making, and partnership activities (CALL TO ACTION ITEM 28: PARK PULSE). Each assessment synthesizes existing scientific data from a variety of

Coral reef and fish at Kaloko-Honokōhau National Historical Park, Hawaii
NPS/JEFFREY CROSS

sources to report on current conditions (and trends where possible), critical data gaps, and resource condition influences for a subset of important park natural resources. As of September 2011, assessment projects and final reports had been completed for 32 NPS units with 20 additional park reports scheduled for completion in 2012.

Vital signs water quality monitoring protocols are in place, and water quality monitoring is being conducted in all 32 I&M networks (CALL TO ACTION ITEM 28: PARK PULSE). The Water Resources program continues to assist the networks with data management and field methods for network water quality monitoring.

The Water Rights Branch supported water resource protection projects in 2011 to collect, process, and analyze streamflow and water level data in seven parks; monitor post-flooding impacts on sediment and riparian resources on the Green and Yampa rivers in **Dinosaur National Monument (CO)**; determine environmental flow needs in three parks; determine aquifer characteristics at **White Sands National Monument (NM)**; investigate the importance of fresh and brackish water on coral reef ecosystems at **Kaloko-Honokōhau National Historical Park (HI)**; and develop engineering data to support a water right application at **Grand Teton National Park (WY)**. More than $650,000 supported these activities and assistance from the Office of the Solicitor in various legal forums to secure and protect water resources.

The Ocean and Coastal Resources Branch was funded for the first time in FY 2010. The program adopted strategies from the 2006 *Ocean Park Stewardship Action Plan* and regional strategic plans for ocean and coastal park stewardship. Technical specialists have been placed in the Southwest, Pacific West, and Alaska regions, and project funds were distributed through the competitive Service-wide Comprehensive Call. Funds supported an investigation of ecosystem responses to increasing nutrients at **Kaloko-Honokōhau and Kalaupapa national historical parks (HI)**; the linkages between toxic red tides, hydrodynamics, and groundwater nutrient fluxes at **Cape Cod National Seashore (MA)**; and other projects listed in Appendix F.

Natural Resource Projects

Natural resource project funding allows parks to address high-priority natural resource management needs beyond the scope of park budgets. Projects fall into the categories of Resource Protection, Natural Resource Preservation Program, Biological Resources–Competitive, Climate Change Response, Natural Sounds, and Water Resources. To ensure that projects address the highest priority needs across the National Park System, projects are evaluated and ranked through the Servicewide Comprehensive Call process.

The Resource Protection program supports projects that propose innovative approaches involving natural resource specialists, protection rangers, researchers, and partners from other agencies to focus on resources at risk. In FY 2011 the Resource Protection program initiated eight projects that addressed natural resource issues such as poached plants, illegal off-road vehicle use, bear mortality, and marijuana cultivation on park lands. A list of Resource Protection projects active in FY 2011 is included in Appendix G.

The Natural Resource Preservation Program (NRPP) supports diverse activities in areas such as wildlife, fisheries, and vegetation management; specialized inventories; planning; mitigation; and restoration. Block grants to regions are an important mechanism for assisting smaller parks in meeting high-priority natural resource needs. NRPP funding is distributed across eight categories (Table 2-7). A list of NRPP projects funded in FY 2011 is included in Appendix H.

Alaska Special Projects allows the National Park Service to undertake projects that improve the protection and management of NPS units in Alaska, which are managed under the Alaska National Interest Lands Conservation Act and other state-specific requirements.

Disturbed Lands Restoration provides funding for parks to restore disturbed lands—lands where natural conditions and processes have been degraded, damaged, or destroyed by development (e.g., facilities, roads, mines, dams) and/or by agricultural practices.

Natural Resource Management projects make up the largest segment of the NRPP. Eligible projects include resource management actions; tactical biological studies; development of new physical science theory, management approaches, and protocols; and combined research and follow-up resource management or mitigation actions.

Regional Program Block Allocation projects improve natural resource knowledge and condition, including projects such as specialized inventories currently outside the scope of the I&M Program and mitigation actions (e.g., fossil inventories and invasive plant or invasive animal control).

Table 2-7. Natural Resource Preservation Program (NRPP) project totals and funding by category, FY 2011

NRPP funding categories	Number of projects	FY 2011 funding ($)
Alaska Special Projects	11	467,000
Disturbed Lands Restoration	9	790,000
Natural Resource Management	39	3,139,000
Regional Program Block Allocation	60	1,303,000
Regional Small Park Block Allocation	54	933,000
Servicewide Projects	12	779,000
Threatened and Endangered Species	11	467,000
Park-Oriented Biological Support	20	202,000
TOTAL[a]	216	8,080,000

[a] $22,500 in NRPP funds were reallocated from Natural Resource Management to Servicewide projects to complete their obligation at the close of FY 2011

Burning non-native Austrian pines to help restore native jack pine and dune habitat and increase prairie warbler nesting opportunities at Sleeping Bear Dunes National Lakeshore, Michigan (NRPP–Regional Program Block project)
NPS PHOTO

The **Regional Small Park Block Allocation** helps small parks achieve their natural resource goals.

Servicewide and Support projects address national priorities and issues that cut across several regions (e.g., air quality, water resources). Some projects are designed to provide prototypes, tools, or capacity that benefit many NPS programs, while others respond to emergency issues.

Threatened and Endangered Species projects are on-the-ground conservation efforts that contribute to the NPS long-term goal to increase the number of park populations of listed species that are making progress toward recovery and to restore these species when they have been extirpated from parks.

The National Park Service and the U.S. Geological Survey (USGS)–Biological Resources Discipline jointly fund USGS biological projects that provide exploratory research and technical assistance for parks. In FY 2011 the National Park Service contributed $201,928 and the USGS contributed $371,559 for these **Park-Oriented Biological Support** projects. In addition, the National Park Service contributed $55,984 of climate change funding for two POBS projects. See Appendix I for a list of projects funded in FY 2011.

Chapter 3: Accomplishments by Region

Seven regions encompass the nearly 400 diverse units of the National Park System. These regions face many of the same broad-scale issues, such as invasive species, energy development, and climate change, as well as issues unique to individual parks or regions. To address these challenges and protect NPS resources, park, regional, network, and servicewide staff work with partners, cooperators, volunteers, and contractors. This chapter includes examples of significant natural resource accomplishments made across the National Park System in FY 2011. While not all inclusive, these projects are representative of the outstanding progress being made in protecting our national parks.

Alaska Region (AKR)

Alaska Region parks stretch from the shores of the Gulf of Alaska to Mount McKinley, the highest peak in North America, to lands north of the Arctic Circle. Many contain vast tracts of wilderness, including relatively pristine ecosystems. Of the 84 million acres of land managed by the National Park Service, nearly 55 million acres are in Alaska. The primary challenge for managers is to provide for appropriate and mandated uses inside and adjacent to parks without compromising the health and integrity of the ecosystems protected within the parks.

High-profile issues confronting Alaskan parks include harvest-level conflicts with state land managers; managing off-highway vehicle use; understanding ecosystem health; responding to evolving climate change scenario planning; balancing visitor use with wildlife concerns; preparing for potential oil spills; gathering adequate baseline information to respond to climate change and mining, oil, and infrastructure development; and understanding emerging threats from issues like white-nose syndrome, invasive species, and ecosystem contaminants. The region is responding to these issues by taking an increasingly issue-based approach to project development, focusing the small pool of available expertise and funding on similar issues at multiple parks.

The *Alaska Natural Resource Program – A Strategy for the Future*, published in February 2011, sets the direction and provides a framework for effective natural resource

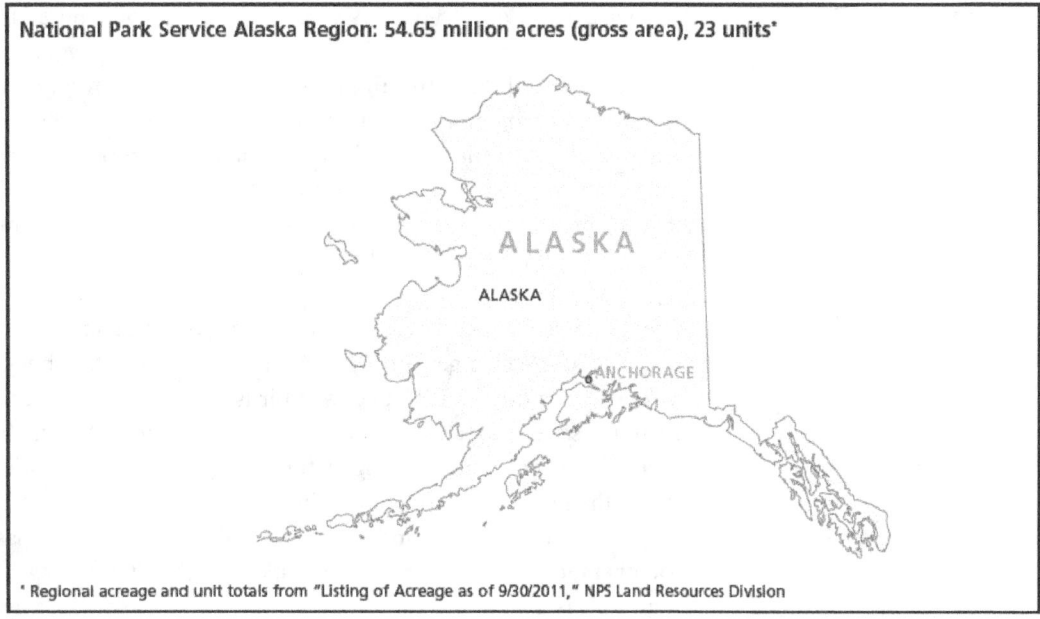

National Park Service Alaska Region: 54.65 million acres (gross area), 23 units*

* Regional acreage and unit totals from "Listing of Acreage as of 9/30/2011," NPS Land Resources Division

Redoubt Volcano in Lake Clark National Park and Preserve, Alaska
NPS/DAN NIOSI

Fish fence installation on the Bartlett River in Glacier Bay National Park and Preserve
NPS PHOTO

management in the region for the next ten years. A companion document will identify specific actions for each of the focus areas developed in the strategy.

Park Accomplishments

Alagnak Wild River: The Alagnak bird survey conducted in June 2011 recorded 78 species. Two of the species (American kestrel and bar-tailed godwit) had not previously been recorded in the site. Sixteen species observed during surveys and previously listed as "probably present" were confirmed. Twenty-four species detected during surveys are designated as species of concern by conservation organizations. CALL TO ACTION ITEM 28: PARK PULSE

Denali National Park and Preserve: Some of the most productive ecosystems in North America, boreal wetlands are the least studied and understood ecosystem in the park. An ongoing project seeks to identify the boreal forest wetland nesting birds that may be negatively affected by wetland loss caused by climate change and serve as a reference for assessing future changes. In 2011 researchers detected more than 50 species of birds, including several species of concern. They documented successful nesting by tundra swans, the first documented breeding record for this species in Denali and one of the only documented nesting records for this species in interior Alaska.

Glacier Bay National Park and Preserve: Fishing on the Bartlett River has increased two-fold over the last decade, but the sustainability of the recreational coho salmon harvest is unknown because no run size information exists. Park staff installed Sonar equipment to collect near-visual-quality sound imagery of migrating fish, which will allow them to estimate coho salmon escapement through 2014. Coho salmon is a species of management concern.

Geologic Resources staff assisted the park with conducting field inventories of Silurian paleontological resources. The fieldwork contributed to a greater understanding of the park's geology and paleontology, including discovery of a new species of fossil brachiopod. Several scientific publications are being prepared to name and describe the new brachiopod and to present the new interpretation of the Silurian geology for the park.

Katmai and Lake Clark National Parks and Preserves: The timing of seasonal biological events (phenology) is an indicator of environmental change. Time-lapse cameras were installed in 2010 at three remote automated weather stations in the parks. Photographs retrieved from the cameras showed thin and often short-lasting snowpacks at the three sites, with green-up lagging snowmelt by as much as two and a half months. Three

Field crew and conservation dog returning to the Great Kobuk Sand Dunes in Kobuk Valley National Park after searching for bear scat
NPS/MARCI JOHNSON

Alaska EPMT crew members preparing for an herbicide treatment near Exit Glacier in Kenai Fjords National Park
NPS/REBECCA THOMPSON

additional cameras were acquired in 2011 to expand and upgrade the existing sites. In 2012 the Southwest Alaska I&M Network will partner with the PhenoCam Network, a collaborator with the USA National Phenology Network, for additional support. CALL TO ACTION ITEM 28: PARK PULSE

Kobuk Valley National Park: Black bears (*Ursus americanus*) in the park occupy part of the northwestern-most edge of their North American range, where they coexist with brown bears and contribute to subsistence, recreation, and wilderness values. Until this project, surveys for black bears had not been undertaken in this region. In 2011 conservation dogs trained to locate bear scat by scent traversed more than 55 kilometers along transects in the tundra and boreal forest adjacent to the Great Kobuk Sand Dunes. DNA samples from each scat will be genotyped to determine the species and identify unique individuals, ultimately providing a measure of bear density and the relative density of brown and black bears in a remote area frequented by backcountry campers. The samples will also be used for general diet analyses. These unique, non-invasive methods and management goals are being shared with residents, visitors, and distance audiences.

Sitka National Historical Park: Staff tested Environment and Natural Resources Institute (ENRI) macroinvertebrate and algae sampling protocols to analyze the stream health of the Indian River. Objectives include sampling macroinvertebrates and algae, applying water quality indexes, and comparing results with previously established index streams. Testing is now complete; results will be used to formulate a long-term sampling strategy for the Indian River. FY 2011 results indicate significant impacts to stream habitat during low-flow events.

Regional Accomplishments

Intensive Management Workgroup: The State of Alaska has increased its efforts to implement the Intensive Management Law of 1994, leading to a growing number of predator control areas adjacent to NPS lands and predator harvest liberalizations on NPS preserves. While these actions may result in impairments, the National Park Service has largely been in a reactive mode. Therefore, a subgroup of the Alaska Leadership Council is drafting regulatory language to address wildlife harvest practices on Alaskan parklands. In addition, a workgroup of NPS staff, university researchers, and State of Alaska staff has been chartered to develop working definitions of the Alaska National Interest Lands Conservation Act terms "natural" and "healthy" and provide guidance on the quantitative and scientific assessment of these terms.

Invasive Plant Management: Alaska parks have a unique opportunity to prevent widespread establishment of invasive plants because current infestation levels are low. Following the *Regional Invasive Plant Management Plan*, the Alaska EPMT implemented an herbicide treatment program in **Kenai Fjords National Park** and **Katmai, Wrangell-St. Elias, and Glacier Bay national parks and preserves**. Initial inspections showed good progress. Using an integrated approach that includes herbicide treatment helps control infestations that have not responded to manual controls. The Alaska EPMT also partnered with the Bristol Bay Native Association to map and control non-native invasive plants in southwest Alaska. Using grant funding, the association hires and trains local residents as invasive plant technicians to lead local outreach, inventories, and control efforts. These technicians have started increasing awareness of the invasive species issue in areas that are still largely invasive free.

Status and Trends of Glaciers: Basic information is lacking on the extent of glaciers and their response to climatic changes in NPS units in Alaska. A project was initiated to document the status and recent trends in the extent of glaciers in the region's nine glaciated parks. Glacier mapping and volume change estimates are complete for **Glacier Bay National Park and Preserve** and progressing on the other parks. Results to date show that the vast majority of glaciers in Glacier Bay and Denali have shrunk considerably, mainly by terminus retreat.

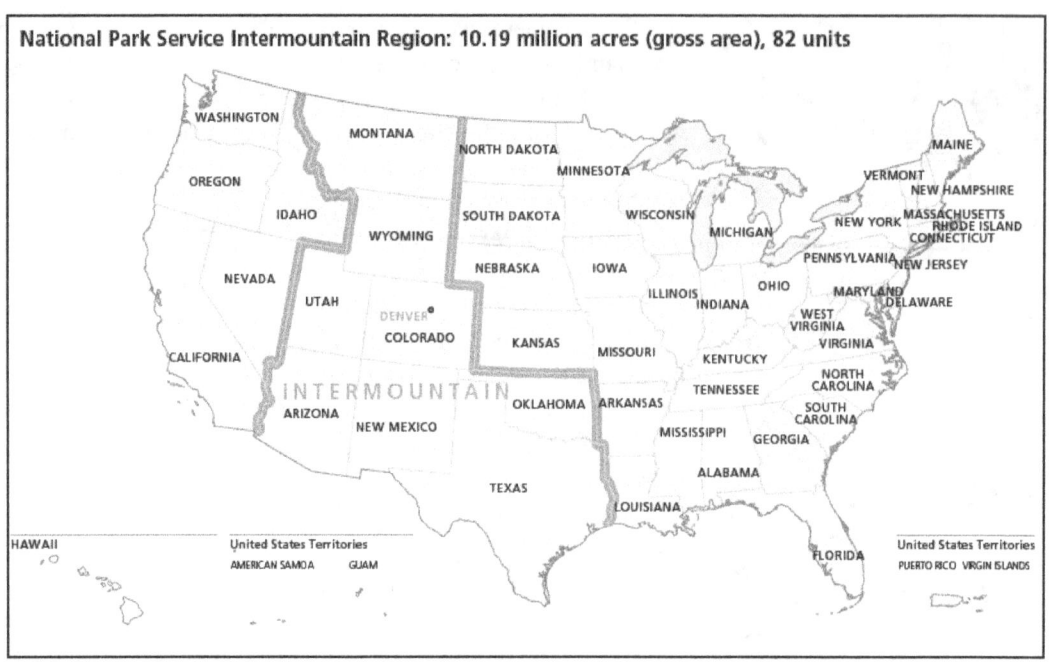

Intermountain Region (IMR)

The Intermountain Region's varied environments—from barrier islands to deserts, prairies to alpine peaks—give rise to an equally diverse collection of NPS sites. The Intermountain Region identified five major focus areas to be addressed by the regional natural resource program: climate change, invasive species, energy development, disturbed lands restoration, and border impacts. These focus areas represent major challenges to almost all parks in the region.

The region's strategy to address these important issues and management challenges includes building partnerships with stakeholders and other agencies; prioritizing ecosystem needs and management responses; and seeking funds for research, monitoring, and management programs that can deliver tangible resource benefits to parks.

Park Accomplishments

Amistad National Recreation Area (TX): Successful breeding of the endangered interior least tern (Sterna antillarum athalassos) was documented during a two-year study. One hundred eighty-three adults produced at least 61 fledglings in 2011. Breeding attempts by adult terns were unsuccessful in 2010 because the islands where the birds nested were inundated with water as the lake rose after Hurricane Alex. This finding indicates that the most critical component of successful breeding is adequate nesting habitat. When adequate habitat is available, the terns at Amistad were successful at raising chicks to fledgling stage.

Chaco Culture National Historical Park (NM): During FY 2011 initial paleontological resource inventory work was completed on 5,215 acres of the park. In total, 99 new fossil features were documented. Eight potential new localities were discovered pending further examination. Park staff also began work on a paleontological resources management plan that will include monitoring protocols and collections guidance. CALL TO ACTION ITEM 28: PARK PULSE

Dinosaur National Monument (CO, UT): Implementation of the park's *Invasive Plant Management Plan* continued. In FY 2011 staff achieved a significant milestone with complete eradication of the last Russian olive (*Elaeangus angustifolia*), an invasive species that can outcompete native vegetation. The park's success has encouraged neighboring BLM and private land owners to work on their Russian olive problems in adjacent areas. A new effort in 2010–2011 included military veterans in the park's volunteer Weed Warrior Program.

Glacier National Park (MT): Warming temperatures are melting ice fields in the park, exposing culturally significant artifacts that are highly vulnerable to degradation and loss. The exposed archeological materials hold information about the prehistory of the Salish, Kootenai, and Blackfeet peoples. In collaboration with tribes and university partners, the park has developed a unique and transferable "ice patch archeology" protocol for collecting culturally sensitive Native American artifacts. Interviews with tribal elders have identified culturally sensitive areas and traditional practices, information that is crucial in establishing the relevance of exposed materials to indigenous communities. Through communication products such an interactive DVD and a documentary, the work is raising awareness of the significance of cultural resources in the park and how climate change is affecting them. CALL TO ACTION ITEM 3: HISTORY LESSON

Grand Teton National Park (WY): The Air Quality program, in conjunction with Colorado State University and the USFS, is conducting the Grand Teton Reactive Nitrogen (RN) Deposition Study to investigate nitrogen deposition pathways in the park. Increases in deposition of RN compounds can adversely affect sensitive ecosystems. The project consisted of a field study to measure and characterize the composition and magnitude of RN deposition, followed by modeling and assessment using the measured and other data to estimate the contributions of sources to the deposited RN. Initial results show that sources of ammonia are the largest contributor to RN; organic nitrogen compounds are also a significant contributor. Project results will provide baseline information about transport and deposition of RN in the park, yield initial source apportionment information, and lay the groundwork for additional future measurements if warranted. CALL TO ACTION ITEM 28: PARK PULSE

Grand Teton National Park (WY) and Yellowstone National Park (ID, MT, WY): The Air Quality program conducted the Greater Yellowstone Area Multi-Agency Air Pollution Effects Workshop in April 2011. The workshop brought together NPS, USFS, USFWS, and State of Wyoming staff and university researchers to discuss the state of the science for air pollution critical loads and ecosystem thresholds and trends for water quality, soils, and aquatic and terrestrial biodiversity in the Greater Yellowstone Ecosystem. Critical loads are an emerging approach within the United States for quantifying the levels of air pollution deposition at which sensitive components of ecosystems are impacted. They are increasingly being used in agency planning and regulatory processes.

Great Sand Dunes National Park and Preserve (CO): In 2008 the Colorado Division of Reclamation, Mining, and Safety identified reclamation alternatives and recommendations for illegal gravel pits and ponds located along Sand Creek. These ponds were stocked

Eradicating the last Russian olive (inset) in Dinosaur National Monument, Colorado and Utah
NPS PHOTO

Applying herbicide treatment to buffelgrass in Saguaro National Park, Arizona, using boom sprayer
NPS PHOTO

California condor
NPS PHOTO

with fish infected with whirling disease. To remove the disease, the ponds had to be removed. ARRA funds were used to reclaim these ponds; earthwork was completed in September 2010. In October 2011, the revegetation project was started with 1,177 narrow leaf cottonwood trees planted in the project area. In the spring of 2012, wetland plants will be planted on the site.

Organ Pipe Cactus National Monument (AZ): The monument's Quitobaquito Pond serves as a refuge for the endangered Rio Sonoyta pupfish (*Cyprinodon eremus*) and the Sonoyta mud turtle (*Kinosternon sonoriense Longifemorale*), which is a candidate for listing. The surface elevation of the pond dropped significantly beginning in 2005, presenting an imminent threat to these species. A multi-year project to stop the leakage causing this decline was completed in FY 2011. The complex restoration effort required moving the pupfish and turtles to temporary holding facilities, clearing vegetation, rehabilitating the pond berm and bottom, sealing the area suspected of leakage, and other actions. The pond is currently holding at its highest stable level since 2005 or earlier.

Saguaro National Park (AZ): Over the past five years, the economic and ecological threats created by the buffelgrass (*Pennisetum ciliare*) invasion in southern Arizona have resulted in serious concerns for the future health of the Sonoran Desert ecosystem. Control activities have not been able to keep pace with the species' rapid expansion. A USFS-funded collaborative project among federal, state, and local governments and universities conducted experiments to evaluate the use of helicopters and specialized equipment (a boom sprayer and a spray ball) to apply herbicide to treat large and remote infestations. Initial analysis seems to indicate that both methods offer effective treatment in steep, saguaro-studded terrain; additional data are being analyzed. The results will inform management for a suite of agencies.

Timpanogos Cave National Monument (UT): In 2011 at least 22,737 visitors out of 90,948 were unable to experience the monument's most significant resource, the Timpanogos Cave System, because of accessibility concerns. To allow for a richer park experience for those who may never be able to visit in person, monument staff worked with Northern Arizona University to develop a visually stunning, descriptive, and stimulating series of podcasts (with descriptive transcripts) for download. These podcasts will offer all visitors, regardless of ability, a chance to experience, share, and understand the significance of the cave system, monument, and surrounding American Fork Canyon. CALL TO ACTION ITEM 17: GO DIGITAL

Zion National Park (UT): Park staff collaborated with various agencies and organizations to provide educational outreach to local citizens regarding the stewardship of California condor populations. They also offered the first non-lead ammunition demonstration events in Utah to protect condors from lead-ingestion poisoning. Lead poisoning is considered the top threat facing the successful reintroduction and conservation of the endangered California condor.

Regional Accomplishments

Climate Change Focus: Understanding the impacts of climate change is critical to the management of natural resources in all IMR parks. To address this need, the region has taken a number of actions. A full-time climate change coordinator, housed in IMR's Climate Change and Landscape Conservation Cooperative program, has been hired. The Climate Change and Sustainability Committee, an IMR steering committee, developed a charter. Staff completed the Climate Change Training Needs Assessment project, which describes the training needs of various disciplines and proposes a competency program.

Earth Science Course: NPS staff participated in the "Earth Science in Context" content course for teachers. The two-week class is offered through the National Science Foundation–funded Rocky Mountain Middle School Math and Science Partnership. Air Quality program staff led lectures and activities on air quality. Geologic Resources and Water Resources staff also gave presentations. Teachers learned about natural resource issues in national parks and took lessons back to their classrooms. CALL TO ACTION ITEM 16: LIVE AND LEARN

Invasive Plant Monitoring Informs Management: Northern Colorado Plateau I&M

Students filming podcast footage in Timpanogos Cave National Monument, Utah
NPS/JONATHAN LOTT

crews showed that park invasive plant control efforts have succeeded in reducing invasive species across monitored sites. These include Canada thistle and black henbane in **Fossil Butte National Monument (WY)**; tamarisk, tree-of-heaven, and Russian knapweed at **Capitol Reef National Park (UT)**; and white horehound at **Golden Spike National Historic Site (UT)**. Where control efforts were not undertaken, the number and size of priority exotic plant infestations have increased along monitoring routes at Fossil Butte in most other areas. Many invasive exotic plants are present in small, localized invasions where there is a promising chance of successful management control and eradication. Monitoring reports have been routinely used by park and EPMT staff for control efforts. CALL TO ACTION ITEM 28: PARK PULSE

Studying Sources of Desert Water: *Tinajas* ("little jars") represent the majority of surface waters in many desert ecosystems. They support both localized aquatic plants and animals and wide-ranging terrestrial species that require direct access to water. Nearly all tinajas were assumed to be fed by runoff following rain events. However, water isotope analyses conducted by the Sonoran Desert I&M Network indicate that a surprisingly large number of perennial tinajas are primarily supported by groundwater—often relatively old (pre-1950s) water. The age of the water suggests that some of these critical habitats are partially buffered from climate change–driven impacts to seasonal patterns of precipitation and highlights their importance for maintaining ecosystem services within park landscapes. CALL TO ACTION ITEM 28: PARK PULSE

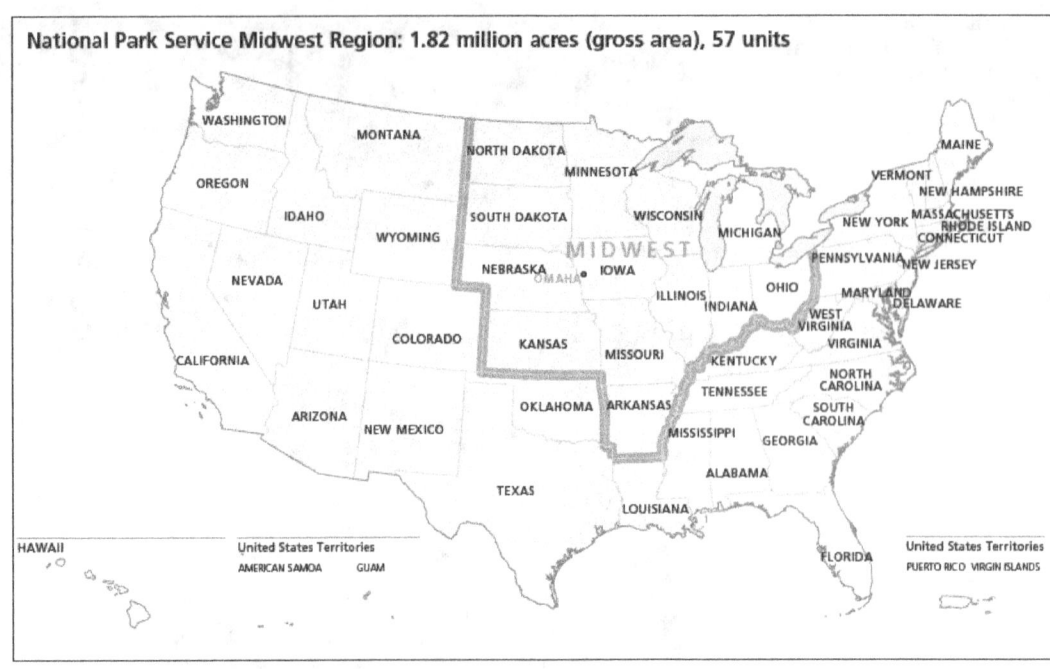

Midwest Region (MWR)

The parks of the Midwest Region contain diverse areas with a rich natural heritage of northern forests, prairie landscapes, southern hardwoods, and wetland, stream, and lake environments. Many of these lands had been farmed, grazed, or logged before becoming part of the National Park System. Therefore, in addition to protecting existing natural resources, a great deal of effort by parks in the region has centered on ecological restoration with a record of success in restoring degraded fish and wildlife habitat. Projects have restored natural plant communities, treated invasive plants, and reintroduced extirpated wildlife.

Continued diligence to deal with emerging threats continues as a high priority so parks can preserve and sustain their existing resources. In FY 2011 wildlife health, forest pests and diseases, ungulate population management, and aquatic nuisance species were among the top priorities for parks in the region.

Park Accomplishments

Apostle Islands National Lakeshore (WI): A new exhibit, "Changing Climate…Changing Cultures," at the Northern Great Lakes Visitor Center identifies the potential effects of climate change on cultures and traditions, focuses on the importance of wild rice production to the Ojibwe culture, and identifies how changes in climate may threaten this traditional way of life. Audiences become aware of how changes in Great Lakes climate affect other aspects of area ecosystems and how choices they make can help mitigate these impacts. The project was a collaborative effort among the National Park Service, USFS, Great Lakes Indian Fish and Wildlife Commission, University of Wisconsin, and Wisconsin Historical Society. CALL TO ACTION ITEM 3: HISTORY LESSON, ITEM 19: OUT WITH THE OLD

Arkansas Post National Memorial (AR): Exotic understory plants outcompete native vegetation, prevent natural regeneration, and severely impact the aesthetics of the park's cultural landscape. Park staff, with the assistance of Youth Conservation Corps members, continued treatment and suppression of invasive exotic vegetation on 1.5 acres of bottomland forest. This action will allow native species to regenerate, enhancing the historic character of the forests and contributing to the accurate representation of the ecologic conditions of the historic periods memorialized at the park.

Badlands National Park (SD): The park contains highly significant mammalian and marine fossils that are at risk to erosion and fossil poaching. In summer 2011, project funding permitted documentation of 13 new paleontological localities. The new sites documented from this project generated further research questions and allowed for the salvage collection of scientifically significant fossils. With the proposed Tribal National Park, park staff are working closely with tribal employees to develop an active paleontology program on the Pine Ridge Indian Reservation.

Herbert Hoover National Historic Site (IA): Park staff are working to increase native plant diversity in an 81-acre reconstructed tallgrass prairie. The prairie is part of the historically significant property and landscape associated with the life of Herbert Hoover. The "desired condition" in the park's general management plan is a facsimile of the native tallgrass prairie that covered much of Iowa, containing relatively few invasive species. Staff planted native spring flowering plants over approximately 10 acres. Once established, these plants will provide a source of seed to collect and later broadcast.

Hopewell Culture National Historical Park (OH): A total of 102 acres have been planted in native vegetation at Hopeton Earthworks since 2003. This year, 79 of those acres were mowed to help maintain these restoration parcels. In FY 2011 natural resource personnel from the park, NPS Midwest Regional Office, and Great Plains CESU collaborated with the University of Nebraska on a research study entitled "Revegetation of Archeological Sites at Hopewell Culture National Historical Park." The study will review pertinent literature on the possible effects of native grass roots on archeological features and, in consideration of these possible effects, identify and evaluate reasonable revegetation alternatives using native and/or non-invasive exotic vegetation for stabilizing earthworks and mounds.

Hot Springs National Park (AR): Ozark chinquapin (*Castanea ozarkensis*) and American chestnut (*Castanea dentata*) trees in the park fell victim to chestnut blight in the early 20th century. An innovative, collaborative project with the Ozark Chinquapin Foundation will reintroduce blight-resistant genetic stock to restore healthy chinquapins to Sugarloaf Mountain in the park. The mountain hosts a community of Ozark chinquapin sprouts but no healthy adults are found within the park boundary. The Heartland I&M Network will help prepare the site, which will be planted by the foundation, and monitor project success.

Jewel Cave National Monument (SD): Jewel Cave is currently the second longest in the world at 157.36 miles and is a popular destination for visitors. The park's resource management staff worked with a contractor to develop a search and rescue pre-plan for 1.7 miles of off-trail routes within the cave. Besides the obvious visitor safety benefit, careful pre-planning will minimize the impacts to

2011 GeoCorp intern at Badlands National Park, South Dakota, with a brontothere skull he discovered
NPS PHOTO

cave resources that would inevitably occur during an actual rescue.

Pea Ridge National Military Park (AR): Heartland I&M Network staff recently discovered Oklahoma salamanders (*Eurycea tynerensis*) in three small, spring-fed streams in the park. This rare salamander is found only from northeastern Oklahoma and southwestern Missouri to extreme northwestern Arkansas. It inhabits undisturbed and thermally constant small woodland streams or spring-brooks. The presence of Oklahoma salamanders in the park indicates that those streams have exceptional water quality. CALL TO ACTION ITEM 28: PARK PULSE

Pictured Rocks National Lakeshore (MI): A 1999–2000 USGS study found that all four species of Unionid mussels in Grand Sable Lake were on the verge of extirpation. Park staff, with assistance from I&M networks, the regional office, and USFWS, instituted a project to determine if the primary fish host for the Elliptio species larvae, yellow perch (*Perca flavesense*), was in decline due to predation by introduced lake trout (*Salvelinus namaycush*) or habitat decline. Surprisingly the study found healthy populations of three of the four species, though concerns still exist about successful reproduction of *Elliptio dilatata*, a species of concern, in the park. Additional results allowed researchers to reject the hypothesis that lake trout predation or other behavioral influences negatively affected yellow perch.

Theodore Roosevelt National Park (ND): In FY 2011 the park implemented its *Elk Management Plan* in an effort to manage the overabundant species. Teams of up to four volunteers, each led by park staff, shot 406 cow elk in the park between November 1, 2010, and January 20, 2011. A total of 181 volunteers participated in reduction activities with no lost-time injuries in 42 field days. Working with North Dakota Sportsmen Against Hunger, the park donated elk meat to community food banks and North Dakota American Indian tribes.

Regional Accomplishments

Indicators of Lake and River Condition: The Great Lakes I&M Network collaborated with the St. Croix Watershed Research Station to use diatoms as bioindicators of lake and river condition in eight network parks. Researchers analyzed diatom communities and geochemistry of sediment cores that dated back to pre-Euro-American settlement times. The analysis showed that most of the sampled lakes showed no changes in estimated pH, total phosphorus, or conductivity over time. Water quality in several lakes changed at the start of farming in the area. In contrast, changes in diatom communities,

Collecting data for a mussel and fish host investigation project in Grand Sable Lake, Pictured Rocks National Lakeshore, Michigan
NPS PHOTO

Prairie dog town, Badlands National Park, South Dakota
NPS PHOTO

sedimentation rates, and geochemistry coincided with Euro-American settlement. Most lakes also showed a recent change in diatom assemblages between approximately 1950 and 2000, many around the 1970s to 1980s. These changes cannot be attributed to land use changes and may be the result of changes in climate. CALL TO ACTION ITEM 28: PARK PULSE

Great Lakes Restoration Initiative: In FY 2011 the region received $4.8 million for nine projects, including funds awarded from a competitive EPA challenge initiative to support jobs for restoration of disturbed sites at **Sleeping Bear Dunes National Lakeshore (MI)**. The initiative resulted in greatly expanded partnerships and multi-agency efforts to perform major restoration projects. Regional aquatic resource specialists were involved in many related projects, including benthic habitat mapping, spill response plans, inventory and ecological surveys, and coastal and fluvial restoration projects.

One Health: Several regional projects addressed wildlife-human diseases in parks following the One Health Program. The University of South Dakota completed a project to investigate five parks for the presence of plague. The National Park Service, USFS, and USFWS cooperated on dusting of prairie dog towns in **Badlands National Park (SD)** and Buffalo Gap National Grassland. This was a collaborative effort to respond to a pervasive non-native disease (plague) that threatens the health of the prairie ecosystem and endangered wildlife species. In FY 2012 the National Park Service will work with USGS to test the effectiveness of an oral plague vaccine for prairie dogs. Black-footed ferrets, reintroduced to prairie ecosystems, are vaccinated for plague. Their offspring, however, remain vulnerable to the disease.

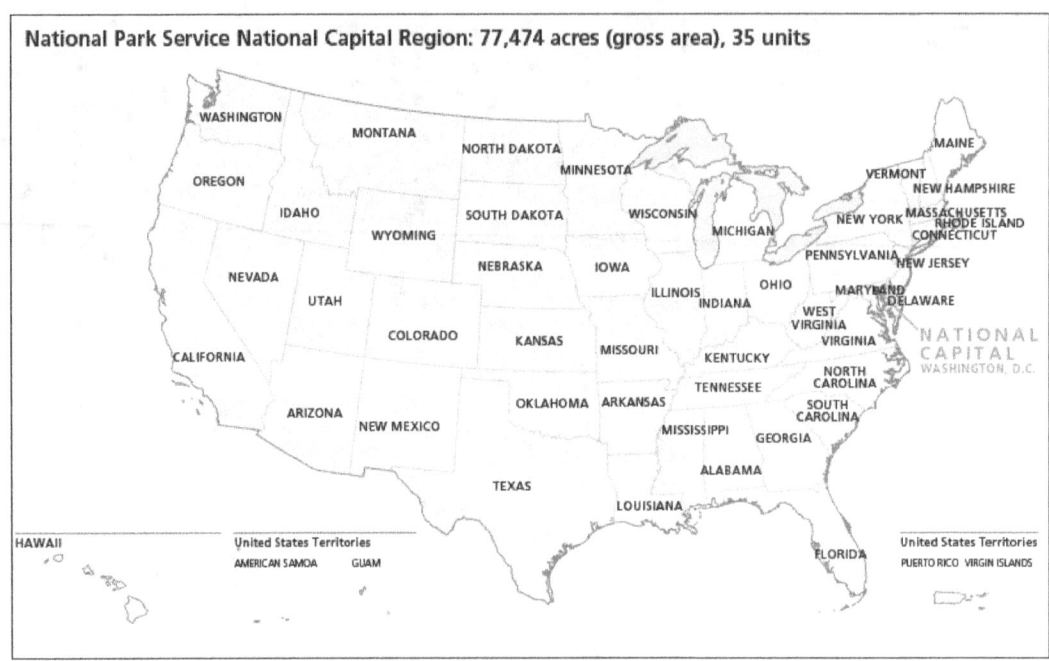

National Capital Region (NCR)

The National Capital Region ranges from the largest contiguous piedmont forest in the National Park System to the national monuments that attract visitors from around the world. Serving more than 40 million visitors annually, the parks feature thousands of historic structures and archeological sites; hundreds of miles of trails, historic canals, and scenic parkways; and large expanses of forest, grassland, and riparian habitats.

The top issues of specific concern to the parks are invasive non-native plant management, overabundant white-tailed deer, and aquatic ecology and water resources. Additionally, the parks are concerned about human-wildlife conflicts, balancing agricultural and natural resource management, urban sprawl and development on park boundaries, native tree sustainability in forests, training interpretive staff in natural resources, and a lack of best management practices for water features.

Park Accomplishments

Antietam National Battlefield (MD): Antietam staff continue to work closely with volunteers to accomplish natural resource projects. The new "Green Brigade" volunteer team assisted with planting native wildflowers and grasses in small riparian and vista areas around the battlefield. Volunteers also continued ongoing riparian buffer improvement and historic woodlot restoration programs. The 10-acre footprint of the East Woods has been completely covered with native hardwood seedlings as part of the ongoing restoration of historic woodlots started in 1995. Additionally, seedlings were planted on the Cunningham Farm riparian buffer along Antietam Creek.

Catoctin Mountain Park (MD): Staff completed a temperature study and baseline water quality inventory of park streams to ascertain if temperature or other variables had impacts on temperature-sensitive brook trout (*Salvelinus fontinalis*) distribution in the park. Brook trout, a species of management concern, were absent from several sites that had suitable temperatures, suggesting that other factors such as sedimentation or competition with other fishes may be affecting them. Recommendations were made for future work and habitat improvement, yielding information about the effect of land management on stream temperature and the impacts of temperature and other factors on the trout population distribution within the park.

Chesapeake and Ohio Canal National Historical Park (DC, MD, WV): Two Geoscientists-in-the-Park volunteers, a hydrologist and a paleontologist, studied wetlands and paleontology in the park. The hydrologist collected data on potential wetland restoration sites and developed a water quality monitoring program. The paleontologist developed a paleontological locality database and identified paleontological sites in the park.

Harpers Ferry National Historical Park (WV): Three volunteer interns from Shepherd University donated 1,200 hours on natural resource projects. They monitored emerald ash borer, an invasive exotic pest; water quality from a sewage plant that flows under park wetlands into the Shenandoah River; and vegetation plots for white-tailed deer impacts. This work would not have occurred without the interns.

Monocacy National Battlefield (MD): The park, working with the NCR Center for Urban Ecology and their Geoscientist-in-the-Park, held a stream assessment and soil and erosion monitoring workshop for NCR natural resource managers, set up a long-term monitoring site, and conducted the initial site survey and year-one follow-up monitoring. Goals for the site include monitoring the rate of change (if any) in channel geometry, monitoring impacts to functioning in-stream macroinvertebrate and fish habitat, and determining the potential for pollution from sediment mobilization. The results will inform management and/or restoration strategies for the stream.

National Capital Parks–East (DC): The parks collaborated with the nonprofit Alice Ferguson Foundation on the Living Shoreline project in Piscataway Park. Approximately one-quarter mile of Potomac River shoreline that can be seen from Mount Vernon was stabilized to prevent further erosion and loss of riparian buffer, maintaining natural aesthetics and protecting cultural resources. Staff contributed to the project planning, adaptive management, permitting, and vegetation monitoring of this project.

Prince William Forest Park (VA): The park is home to the federally threatened and state endangered small-whorled pogonia (*Isotria medeoloides*). In FY 2011 park staff began implementing strategies from its *Isotria Management Plan*, which helps the park address questions about the species' population growth and decline. Staff surveyed 21 known sites twice in 2011 and collected data on invasive species and insect and deer herbivory. Staff also used two techniques—tomato plant cages and PVC/netting—to create low-profile and removable deer exclosures to determine if these methods will improve overall health and fruiting by reducing deer herbivory. The park will continue to investigate new strategies to improve the orchid's habitat and recurrence within the park.

Rock Creek Park (DC): According to Executive Order 13508: Chesapeake Bay Protection

Downloading data to determine the effects of temperature and other variables on brook trout in Catoctin Mountain Park, Maryland
NPS PHOTO

and Restoration, national parks and other federal agencies have a responsibility to reduce the amount of sediment and nutrients flowing into Chesapeake Bay. Regenerative stormwater conveyance is an effective method for rebuilding stream channels to adequately handle increased stormwater runoff from urban development. Park staff worked closely with the DC Department of the Environment to complete an EPA-funded project to install such conveyances in the park. Re-engineering of the stream reduces stormwater velocity, captures sediment and nutrients, and allows more water to infiltrate into the ground. These improvements restore stream function while improving benthic habitat and increasing biodiversity. Fewer sediments and nutrients and less stormwater runoff flow into creeks and Chesapeake Bay, which will help improve the health of the bay.

Several meadow areas in Rock Creek Park provide a transition between open lawn areas and forested areas, offering more habitat diversity for plants and animals. In recent years, visitors are seeing these meadow areas overrun with invasive non-native plants. While working to treat these areas, park staff updated two brochures about the importance of meadows in the park and the problem of invasive plants. The invasive plant brochure explains why they are a problem and offers native species alternatives for planting.

Regional Accomplishments

Forest Vegetation Monitoring: The National Capital Region I&M Network continued its second year of forest vegetation monitoring, visiting 100 plots originally surveyed in 2007. The network now monitors more than 17,500 individual trees, saplings, and seedlings representing 94 species and more than 2,700 shrubs and shrub seedlings representing 39 species. In addition, network staff monitor 27 exotic herbaceous species. Of the plots, 262 (63 percent) contain at least one exotic herbaceous species. Long-term findings will help managers understand the dynamics of network forests and shed light on the impacts of stressors.
CALL TO ACTION ITEM 28: PARK PULSE

Lichen Inventory and Air Quality Analysis: A researcher at George Mason University conducted a lichen inventory in National Capital Region I&M Network parks, identifying 45 species of bark-inhabiting lichens and establishing 102 permanent lichen study plots. Results of analysis for levels of mercury,

Completed stormwater conveyance on Millhouse Tributary in Rock Creek Park, DC, and stream condition before the project (inset)
NPS PHOTO

Rock Creek Park brochures discussing the importance of meadows and the threat of invasive species

copper, lead, zinc, nickel, cadmium, chromium, and sulfur show that the region is home to relatively pollution-tolerant lichen communities and that pollution-sensitive species are uncommon. CALL TO ACTION ITEM 28: PARK PULSE

White-Tailed Deer Management: Managing white-tailed deer is a priority for NCR parks. White-tailed deer management plans/environmental impact statements are underway for Rock Creek Park (DC) and Antietam National Battlefield (MD), Manassas National Battlefield Park (VA), and Monocacy National Battlefield (MD). Staff at Wolf Trap National Park for the Performing Arts (VA) continued a deer monitoring program, installed a 2,500 square foot exclosure to study the impacts of an overabundant deer population on plants, and began other foundation work for the development of a deer management program. During the second year of implementing Catoctin Mountain Park's (MD) *White-tailed Deer Plan*, deer meat from removed animals was donated to local food banks.

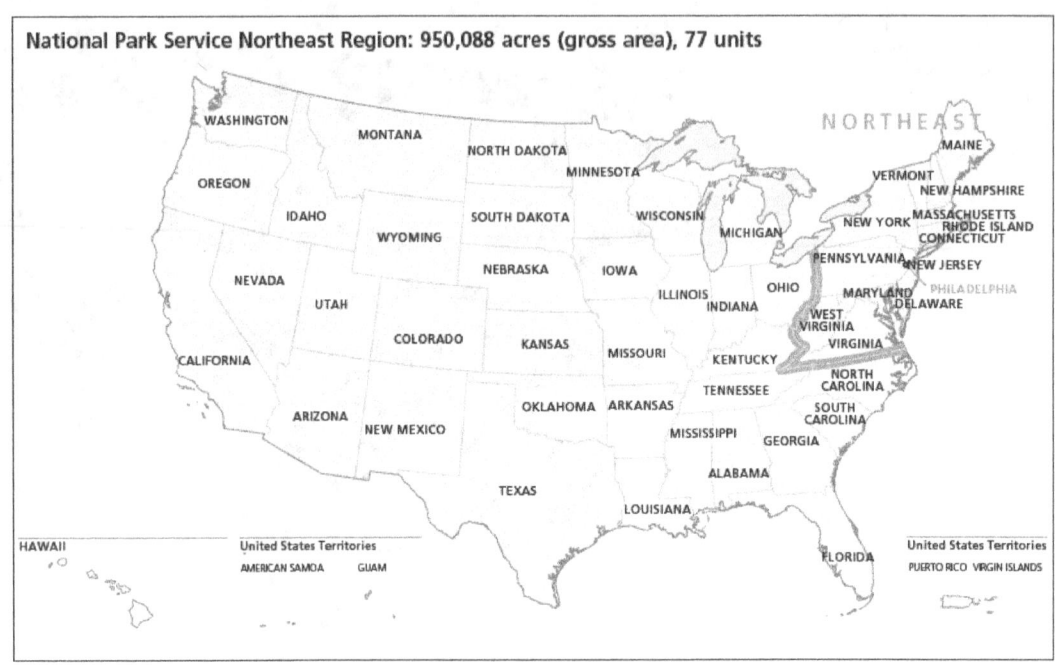

Northeast Region (NER)

The parks of the Northeast Region preserve not only the story of our nation's beginnings but also outstanding natural resources from salt marshes and seashores to rolling hills and granite mountain peaks. Issues of concern for the Northeast Region are climate change and adaptation, energy development, wetland restoration, invasive species, and forest health, among others.

Park Accomplishments

Appalachian National Scenic Trail (ME to GA): The Appalachian Trail MEGA-Transect Project is a tool for examining environmental changes along the more than 2,000 miles of the trail. Several research projects are underway, including a cooperative effort to establish the status and susceptibility of publicly managed lands along the trail—including Delaware Water Gap National Recreation Area (NJ), Shenandoah National Park (VA), and Great Smoky Mountains National Park (NC, TN)—to acidic deposition. The high elevation, ridge-top ecosystems that comprise much of the trail corridor are extremely sensitive and can provide an early indication of environmental effects. In FY 2011 regional and park staff, volunteers, and investigators from USGS, USFS, private institutions, and universities collected water, vegetation, atmospheric deposition, and soil samples that will be used to establish baseline status along the trail and project necessary pollution reductions to promote ecosystem health. The study serves as an example of how the National Park Service can use the trail itself as a MEGA-transect to evaluate environmental change across a sensitive corridor that includes most of the eastern states. CALL TO ACTION 28: PARK PULSE

Cape Cod National Seashore (MA): The GPS SWAT Team teaches GPS mapping and navigation skills and helps address park mapping needs. In FY 2011 the team mapped native fucoid macroalgal mats on Hatches Harbor marsh. Preliminary evidence indicated that the fucoids play a major role in reducing erosion and stabilizing creek banks in northern temperate salt marshes. GPS field surveys of the extent, depth, and fragmentation of these macroalgal mats contribute to understanding how widespread and accurate this characterization is both within and among different marshes and are a component of further research into their ecological function.

Delaware Water Gap National Recreation Area (NJ): Two copper mine shafts dating from the early 1900s historically have been used by various hibernating bat species, including little brown bat, northern long-eared bat, and eastern pipistrelle. The sites are also in the historic range of the federally endangered Indiana bat (*Myotis sodalis*). Barriers to prevent human entry had proven ineffective. As the fragile bat populations are at severe risk from white-nose syndrome, which was documented in both sites in 2009, staff have undertaken an intensive effort to protect bat hibernacula within the park and prevent human access. In FY 2011 staff removed the ineffective barriers and permanently sealed the entrances with bat gates meeting Bat Conservation International design standards. Sealing will prevent human disturbance and help quarantine the spread of the disease by unknowing human carriers.

Fire Island National Seashore (NY): The park has undertaken a project to construct and periodically maintain an erosional head along the bayside shoreline adjacent to the Sailors Haven Marina to restore bayside sediment transport processes interrupted due to dredging and shoreline armoring. During FY 2011 pre-construction ecological monitoring was completed. This demonstration project will provide park managers with information on the bayside physical processes necessary to develop an integrated approach to managing anthropogenically derived erosion along the bayside shoreline.

Saugus Iron Works National Historic Site (MA): In partnership with the Massachusetts Division of Marine Fisheries and the Saugus River Watershed Council, population monitoring for spawning rainbow smelt and American eel was conducted again in 2011. In addition, park natural resource staff coordinated the first year of a two-year project to document the exact locations of rainbow smelt spawning habitat through an egg survey. This project involved community volunteers as well as partner agency staff. The long-term effort to understand and protect these species of management concern will continue in February 2012.

Regional Accomplishments

Effects of Sea-Level Change and Storm Surge: Regional GIS and park natural resource staff at 10 parks are working with the University of Rhode Island Environmental Data Center to identify resources that will be affected by sea-level change and storm surge based on different physical models. The objective of this project is to develop precise elevations for highly valued park resources so that the results of current and future sea-level rise models can be used for local decision making. Project staff established the Monumentation Network, evaluating more than 7,000 candidate geodetic monuments and selecting 500 to retain for long-term NPS records. In addition, 15 new geodetic monuments were installed at **Cape Cod National Seashore (MA)**, **Acadia National Park (ME)**, and **Gateway National Recreation Area (NY)**, and models were run for sea-level rise and storm surge for **Boston**

Field site in Cape Cod National Seashore, Massachusetts, showing geodetic-grade GPS base station
USGS/CHERYL HAPKE

View from Grandview Rim Trail, New River Gorge National River, West Virginia
NPS/DAVID BIERI

Harbor Islands National Recreation Area (MA), Cape Cod, and Acadia.

Climate Change: The Northeast Region published its *Climate Change Strategy and Action Plan*, which is an interdisciplinary document to accomplish goals in four integrated components: science, adaptation, mitigation, and communication. In FY 2011, recognizing the importance of climate change and in support of the servicewide goal of sustainability, the regional director established a Regional Environmental Management System Team to help implement the goals of the regional plan and the NPS *Green Parks Plan*. CALL TO ACTION ITEM 23: GO GREEN

Integrated Pest Management: The regional Integrated Pest Management (IPM) Program addressed issues relating to museums, public health, agriculture, forest resources, landscapes, invasive animals, and plants. Regional staff worked with **Fire Island National Seashore (NY)** to begin a process to define their mosquito management options and worked with the surrounding county mosquito management officials to integrate efforts where possible. Telnet training was developed to keep park and regional staff informed of the IPM issue of bedbugs in the Northeast.

Invasive Insects: During FY 2011 two significant invasive forest insects dispersed or were discovered in the region—the emerald ash borer and the Asian long-horned beetle. So far, only **New River Gorge National River (WV)** has found emerald ash borer in its ash trees, and it is likely that this insect will soon reach many of the parks in the region that have ash trees. The Asian long-horned beetle has become established in Massachusetts and is considered a possible threat to parks in the Boston area and the forests of New England. Both species are very difficult to manage at the landscape scale. With regional funding and forest suppression dollars from the USFS, staff in each Boston-area park have or will receive training on forest insect identification, monitoring, and management.

Phenology Protocol: The Northeast Temperate I&M Network continued to develop an integrated phenology monitoring program. Phenology is the study of the timing of recurrent biological events, such as flowering, leaf out, or animal migration, and is a key indicator of climate change impacts. The network's monitoring program seeks to interest and educate park visitors and volunteers in simple natural history observation, while at the same time providing monitoring data on phenological changes of key plant and animal species in network parks. In collaboration with several organizations, including the USA National Phenology Network, 2011 was the third year of a pilot project to develop methods and begin implementation of volunteer and automated collection of phenology data. Thus far, eight of the 13 Northeast Temperate Network parks are participating or plan to participate in this program. CALL TO ACTION ITEM 28: PARK PULSE

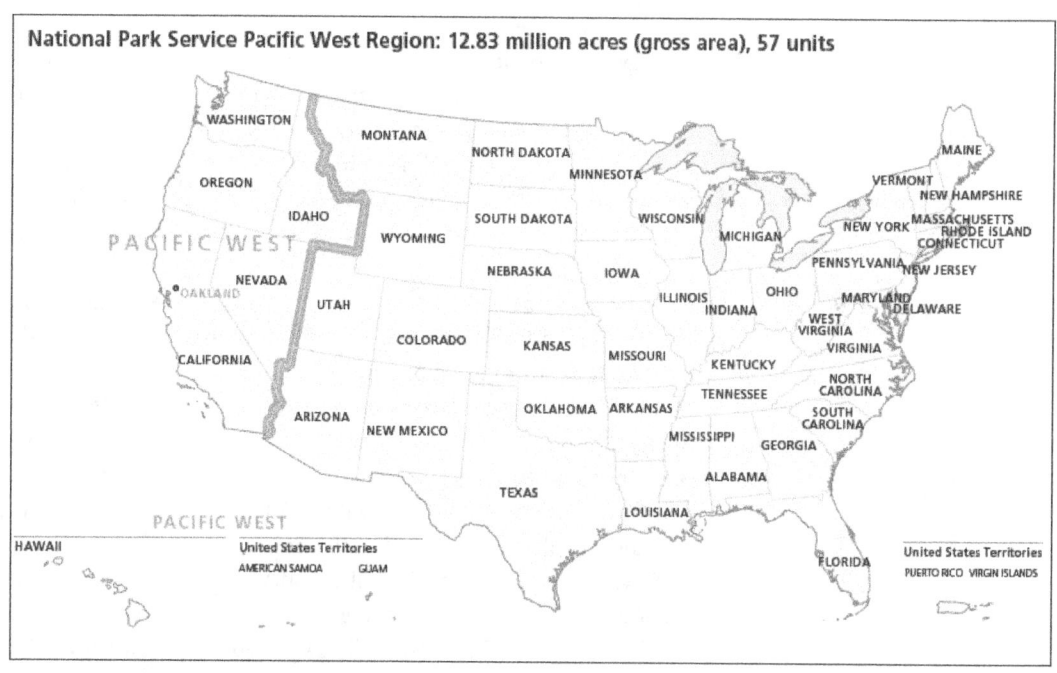

Pacific West Region (PWR)

Rich in cultural and natural diversity, the Pacific West Region extends across more than 100 degrees longitude, encompassing a network of NPS units from eastern Nevada to Guam and Saipan on the other side of the International Date Line. Natural resource issues of concern to the region include fragmentation of ecosystems, preservation of rare and endangered species, climate change, ocean stewardship, invasive exotic species, and air toxics including mercury. The region's strategy to address these difficult resource issues includes building partnerships with stakeholders and other agencies and seeking funds for research, monitoring, and management programs designed to maximize natural resource protection and ecosystem resilience.

Park Accomplishments

Golden Gate National Recreation Area (CA): Efforts continued to enhance habitat for the federally endangered Mission blue butterfly (*Icaricia icarioides missionensis*). A multi-year project is scientifically testing two treatment methods—burning and vegetation removal/soil scraping—to enhance the lupine habitat the butterflies depend upon. In FY 2011 post-treatment vegetation and photo monitoring of the plots was completed. Preliminary observations indicate that both treatments were effective in stimulating regeneration of lupine. Following the outreach plan, staff developed a Mission blue butterfly brochure, updated park and partner websites, and supported events related to the Mission blue butterfly Species of the Year campaign.

Kaloko-Honokōhau and Kalaupapa National Historical Parks (HI): Recent investigations at Kaloko-Honokōhau demonstrated that sub-marine groundwater discharges large volumes of nutrient-laden freshwater to coastal areas, which increases the potential for nuisance algal growth and adversely affects coral reefs. Herbivory may control some of the increased algal growth, but large herbivores have been greatly reduced by intensive fishing. An ongoing project examines the response of algae to nutrient inputs, effects of herbivores on algal growth, influence of herbivore abundance and biomass on algal and coral composition, and potential for managing herbivores to reduce algal biomass and improve coral reef health. The project compares impacts at Kaloko-Honokōhau, an increasingly urbanized park, and Kalaupapa, a relatively remote park.

Pinnacles National Monument (CA): Lead poisoning continues to threaten the reintroduction and conservation of endangered California condors. A study designed to systematically investigate the sources of lead exposure and poisoning provided rigorous quantification that spent lead rifle ammunition fragments are the primary source responsible for lead poisoning frequently documented in condors. Additional potential lead sources were found to represent a small fraction of exposure sources. Results will contribute directly to education, outreach, and management efforts to reduce lead pathways to condors and other wildlife. To address lead toxicity and other general healthcare needs in condors, a new Mobile Condor Care Unit greatly enhances the level of care for birds that must undergo extended treatment.

Pinnacles staff finished a three-year project to restore the bottomlands of a newly acquired ranch. The goal was to bring 80 acres of highly degraded and infested monoculture of yellow star thistle (*Centaurea solstitialis* L.) under more manageable control. A team of interdisciplinary experts implemented an IPM approach using prescribed burns; broadcast herbicide treatment; goat grazing; hand mowing, hoeing, and pulling with youth corps and inmate crews; and spot spraying. Monitoring plots tracked the efficacy of treatment. The community and other land managers have requested that the staff share its lessons learned.

Point Reyes National Seashore (CA): In May 2010 marine protected areas (MPAs) were implemented adjacent to and within the seashore to benefit marine fish and invertebrate populations and potentially offer indirect benefits for fisheries outside the MPAs. A project with the State of California, Pacific States Marine Fisheries Commission, and California Sea Grant used remotely operated vehicles to conduct baseline surveys of marine fish and invertebrates. The combination of before (2009) and after (2011) surveys along with treatment (MPA) and non-treatment (no MPA) sites are providing a robust species list and species numbers. These surveys will be essential for assessing how the MPAs may enhance fish abundance, biodiversity, and size within the MPAs.

The *Bear Valley Visitor Center Lighting Retrofit Guide* was developed in partnership with NPS staff and the California Lighting Technology Center at the University of California, Davis. The guide communicates recommendations for energy-efficient lighting and controls for the visitor center. The general design guidelines could be applied as a model for other NPS visitor centers and museums. The project helps Point Reyes meet federal energy mandates and its Climate Friendly Park Action Plan emission reduction goal. CALL TO ACTION ITEM 23: GO GREEN

Pu'uhonua o Hōnaunau National Historical Park (HI): Geologic Resources staff coordinated with a USGS emeritus geologist to help assess the vulnerability of coastal cliffs impacted by wave action that threatens the main trail in the park. The project included a site visit and associated report with a discussion of the geologic hazards and

Treating Mission blue butterfly plot with fire in Golden Gate National Recreation Area, California
NPS PHOTO

American Conservation Experience crews removing tarps from areas formerly dominated by reed canarygrass in Sequoia and Kings Canyon National Parks
NPS/JONATHAN HUMPHREY

recommendations for long-term management of the trail. Staff also provided information on state requirements for beach nourishment and methods to assess sediment compatibility after a tsunami in March caused dramatic beach erosion that led to exposure of burial sites.

San Juan Island National Historical Park (WA): Park staff organized the Island Prairie Symposium to bring together technical experts and the community to highlight the value of island prairie restoration. Panel members came from a wide variety of backgrounds and organizations, including a local farmer; a historian; the Samish Tribe; National Park Service (I&M, EPMT); USFWS; University of Washington; Nature Conservancy; and Washington Department of Fish and Game. More than 80 community members attended the event.

Sequoia and Kings Canyon National Parks (CA): Park staff continued the fight against invasive reed canarygrass (*Phalaris arundinacea*). They treated 81 acres and reduced the infested area (acres with 100 percent cover) from 7.6 to 0.2 acres. They continued working with 20 private landowners in Wilsonia to conduct control efforts; the success of the project has been noted by many residents not initially supportive. American Conservation Experience crew members assisted with the project. In areas where reed canarygrass has been effectively controlled, staff planted 14,520 native wetland plants.

Whiskeytown National Recreation Area (CA): Deteriorating logging roads and associated trails in the Paige-Boulder Watershed in the park are shedding large quantities of sand into lower Clear Creek, which is critical habitat for threatened Chinook salmon and steelhead trout. The watershed's highly erodible soils and potential for debris flows and human injury make it the park's highest priority for restoration. In FY 2011 the park developed a comprehensive restoration plan for the watershed, providing a blueprint to methodically address restoration of the entire watershed in the most cost-effective manner.

Regional Accomplishments

Assessment of Birds in Sierra Nevada Parks: The Institute for Bird Populations assessed the distribution, abundance, potential effects of ecological stressors, and conservation opportunities for 145 bird species that commonly occur in **Sequoia and Kings Canyon National Parks (CA)**, **Yosemite National Park (CA)**, and **Devils Postpile National Monument (CA)**. Trends declined for 13 species and increased for four. Factors associated with the decline are predominantly related to activities outside of parks, including habitat

Post-doctoral student setting up phenological monitoring of a Joshua tree at Joshua Tree National Park, California
NPS/BRIAN HAGGERTY

degradation or loss from logging, livestock grazing, exurban development, or agricultural conversions. Other factors may include the loss of historic fire regimes, nest parasitism by brown-headed cowbirds, disease, loss of wintering grounds in Central or South America, and contaminants. At a regional scale, most of these species have shown northward and sometimes inland shifts in their centers of abundance since the 1960s, suggesting they are already responding to a warming climate. CALL TO ACTION ITEM 28: PARK PULSE

International Transboundary Water Quality Monitoring: North Coast and Cascades I&M Network staff worked with the British Columbia Ministry of the Environment; Ministry of Forests, Lands, and Natural Resource Operations; and Hope Mountain Center to establish an international transboundary water quality monitoring program for the upper Skagit Watershed in the United States and Canada. The Skagit River is the second largest river in Washington, supporting all the native salmon, trout, and char species found in the Northwest and the largest wintering population of bald eagles in the conterminous United States. CALL TO ACTION ITEM 28: PARK PULSE

Science Communication: The North Coast and Cascades Science Learning Network populated its science gateway website with information about the North Coast and Cascades I&M Program and nine "Science Minute Videos" showing scientists in the field. Production began on eight more videos, which will be completed early in 2012. Staff also produced a 90-page book highlighting the I&M program in lively, non-technical language and helped produce a 15-minute film on climate change, "Inches of Snow and Tide." CALL TO ACTION ITEM 17: GO DIGITAL

Using Phenology to Assess Climate Change Response: A coordinated project involving California national parks supports widespread and consistent monitoring of seasonal shifts in biological events, such as flowering, leaf-out, insect emergence, and animal migration, while promoting citizen science education. Project leads established a scientific framework to guide park-based phenological monitoring and engaged park staff and botanical experts in a species selection process for monitoring in 19 California parks. Phenological monitoring was designed and field-tested for more than 500 individual plants representing 27 species across seven pilot parks. To make these protocols usable for other California national parks, a suite of tools are now available, including methods, maps, photos, species descriptions, education guides, and a report summarizing opportunities for developing phenology-based climate change interpretation, education, and citizen science programs.

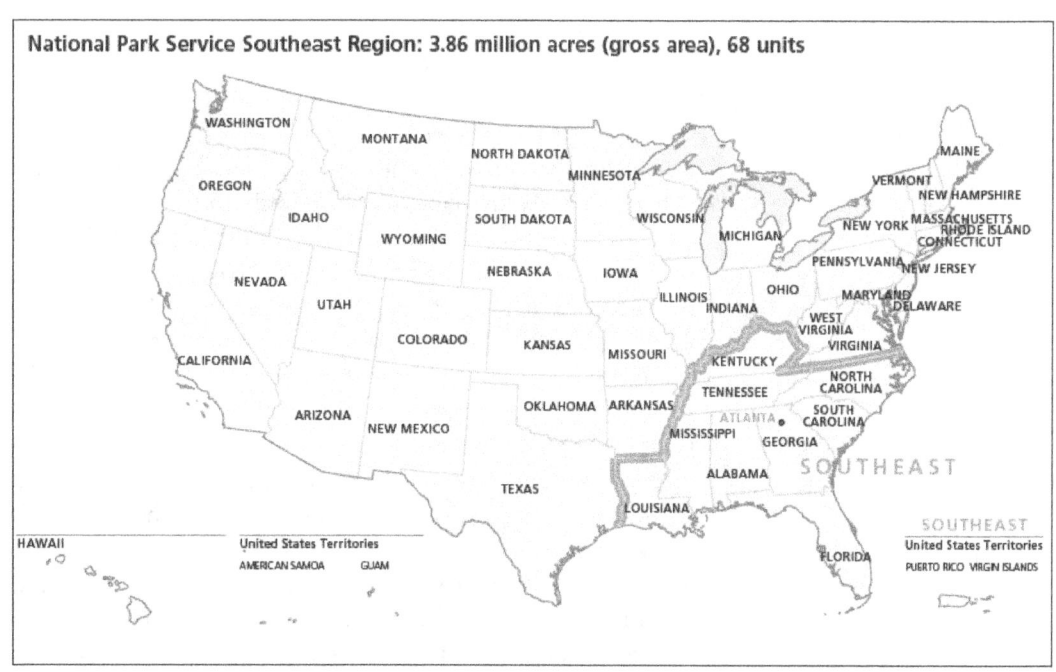

National Park Service Southeast Region: 3.86 million acres (gross area), 68 units

Southeast Region (SER)

While two-thirds of the NPS units in the Southeast Region feature history as their primary theme, the region's natural treasures include biodiversity hotspots in the Great Smoky Mountains and Everglades and five of 10 national seashores.

Park Accomplishments

Big Cypress National Preserve (FL): Florida panthers (*Puma concolor coryi*) are one of world's rarest carnivores, with fewer than 170 individuals in the wild. While numbers vary slightly each year, Big Cypress supports a population of approximately 35 panthers. Radio-collaring and sampling are used to help monitor population dynamics and health and provide information to guide management actions, assess responses to natural events and human-caused impacts, and enhance panther recovery. In FY 2011 the Big Cypress panther team, assisted by Wildlife Health program veterinarians, captured eight adults and visited five dens to mark 13 of 15 known kittens. Twenty-two years of panther survey and monitoring, 15 years of panther reproductive assessment, and nine years of panther capture work help managers more thoroughly understand panther ecology and promote protection of the species.

Big South Fork National River and Recreation Area (KY, TN): American Recovery and Reinvestment Act funds are being used to plug and perform surface reclamation at 39 orphaned well sites. This multi-year project, in conjunction with projects to plug and reclaim an additional 14 orphaned well sites, will remove a long-standing resource and visitor protection problem. In addition, 37 abandoned coal mine entrances were closed. Where the mines provide good habitat for bats, bat-friendly gates were installed to allow bats to enter and exit while keeping the public safely outside. Where habitat is not an issue, polyurethane foam plugs were constructed in the mine entrances, covered by a minimum of a three-foot-deep earthen backfill. Geologic Resources staff provided contract specifications for the well plugging and mine closures, as well as onsite and remote assistance to park staff responsible for oversight.

Buck Island Reef National Monument (Virgin Islands): Four federally listed species of sea turtles nest and/or forage at the monument: hawksbill (*Eretmochelys imbricata*), green (*Chelonia mydas*), loggerhead (*Caretta caretta*), and leatherback (*Dermochelys coriacea*). In addition to recording sea turtle activity, staff and Student Conservation Association interns prepared for a joint NPS and USGS project to track nesting hawksbill and green turtles using satellite transmitters. Tracking the turtles provides a clearer understanding of how nesting females use the waters and coral reefs surrounding the monument during nesting and how they disperse back to their foraging grounds from Puerto

Rico to islands in the eastern Caribbean. CALL TO ACTION ITEM 22: SCALING UP

Canaveral National Seashore (FL): Researchers are analyzing the importance of ephemeral wetlands in maintaining reptile and amphibian biodiversity. Little is known about freshwater swales, the only naturally occurring freshwater wetlands in the seashore, yet more than 50 percent of the seashore's reptile and amphibian species are associated with them. An intensive study seeks to determine which swales contain the highest levels of species diversity, whether swales represent isolated habitats or are acting as a "metapopulation," and what impacts feral hogs are having on amphibians and reptiles in these habitats. In FY 2011 researchers used acoustical recording devices to sample breeding events in swales. Project results will help managers determine the actions needed to maintain current levels of biodiversity at these sites.

Great Smoky Mountains National Park (NC, TN): Researchers from the New York Botanical Garden and Rancho Santa Ana Botanic Garden of Claremont, California, discovered many new lichen records for the park. During 2011 their research emphasis was on the xeric (dry) slopes and cliffs of the west end of the park. The total number of lichen species in the park reached 804 by August 2011; subsequent explorations revealed additional taxa that also appear to be new for the park. There appear to be more lichen taxa documented from the Smokies than any other U.S. national park. CALL TO ACTION ITEM 28: PARK PULSE

Little River Canyon National Preserve (AL): Six miles of the 16-mile DeSoto Scout Trail within the preserve had been abandoned and were not maintained. To address visitors' desire for a longer trail in the preserve, NPS employees spearheaded an effort to rehabilitate the trail, starting with a social media page for the project. Volunteers contributed hundreds of hours of trail work, allowing the park to hold a work and hike day on the trail for Public Lands Day. Several volunteers have since "adopted" the trail to keep it maintained. CALL TO ACTION ITEM 17: GO DIGITAL

Mammoth Cave National Park (KY): The Mammoth Cave International Center for Science and Learning coordinated an International Bat Night celebration in the park in August 2011. This celebration tied in with the United Nation's International Year of the Bat and celebrations across the globe on the same day. Approximately 1,000 people attended the all-day event, which included a variety of bat-related activities—information tables, posters describing current research, junior ranger activities, and using night vision equipment to

A litter of Florida panthers at Big Cypress National Preserve, Florida
PHOTO COURTESY OF RALPH ARNWOOD

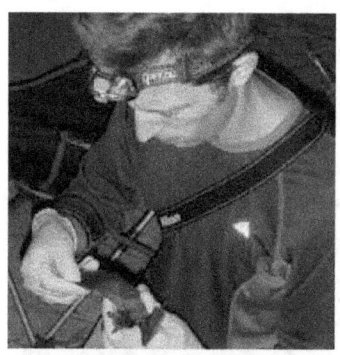

Researcher examining a Rafinesque's big-eared bat (*Corynorhinus rafinesquii*) at Mammoth Cave National Park, Kentucky
NPS/SHANNON TRIMBOLI

watch the bats exiting the cave and bat detectors to hear the bats calling as they flew overhead. CALL TO ACTION ITEM 16: LIVE AND LEARN

Park staff completed a three-year project to protect and propagate populations of wild ginseng (*Panax quinquefolius*) and goldenseal (*Hydrastis canadensis*). Populations of both plants are at risk due to illegal poaching activity associated with the medicinal wild herb trade. In FY 2011, 12 high-density ginseng and goldenseal populations were identified containing over 12,400 plants. Park staff and Student Conservation Association interns planted 571 mature seeds, marked 450 roots with detectable dye, installed 13 remote sensors/cameras, and produced an updated GIS predictive habitat model for both species. Over the course of the project, staff located a total of more than 21,000 individual plants in the field, planted 5,401 mature seeds, and marked 1,750 roots with detectable dye.

Regional Accomplishments

Salt Marsh Collaboration: The Southeast Coast I&M Network worked closely with National Oceanic and Atmospheric Administration (NOAA) National Estuarine Research Reserves, USGS, Northeast Coastal and Barrier I&M Network, and USFWS to develop a common salt marsh community monitoring protocol and data standards including collaborative testing of installation methods and equipment. In addition, the Southeast Coast Network, in collaboration with Guana Tolomato Matanzas National Estuarine Research Reserve staff, located and installed 18 salt marsh elevation/community monitoring stations. The reserve encompasses the administrative boundaries of **Fort Matanzas National Monument (FL)**. CALL TO ACTION ITEM 28: PARK PULSE

Wildlife Monitoring: Monitoring for landbird and amphibian communities is now complete for all 17 Southeast Coast I&M Network parks. The project consisted of almost 10,000 bird observations and analysis of more than 88,000 minutes of audio recordings. These efforts resulted in the addition of nearly 70 species to the parks' species lists: 44 species of birds, 13 amphibians, and 12 reptiles. Several of the new birds included species considered to be conservation priorities by the South Atlantic Migratory Bird Initiative. CALL TO ACTION ITEM 28: PARK PULSE

Chapter 4: Servicewide Accomplishments

By focusing on the broad issues, such as climate change, ocean stewardship, biodiversity, and energy development, that affect resources throughout the National Park System, servicewide natural resource programs reach across state and regional boundaries to provide benefits for multiple parks and regions.

Assessing Resource Vulnerability: Responding to the challenge of climate change requires managers to understand which resources and ecosystems are most vulnerable to changing conditions. The National Park Service collaborated with the National Wildlife Federation and 20 authors from federal agencies, universities, and non-governmental organizations to publish *Scanning the Conservation Horizon*, a vulnerability assessment guide for resource management planning and adaptation. Two detailed park assessments were completed this year—landscapes and wildlife habitat at **Point Reyes National Seashore (CA)** and coastal hazard analysis at **Puʻukoholā Heiau National Historic Site and Kaloko-Honokōhau National Historical Park (HI)**. A third assessment was completed for **Olympic National Park (WA)** in collaboration with the USFS. The National Park Service completed its first vulnerability assessment to address both natural and cultural resources in **Badlands National Park (SD)**, which will serve as an example for future integrated climate change vulnerability assessments across the country. CALL TO ACTION ITEM 28: PARK PULSE

Climate Change Training and Education: The Interpretation and Education and Natural Resource Stewardship and Science directorates joined with the NPS Mather Training Center and NPS National Education Council to create and implement a training module for front-line interpreters and educators that establishes a new standard for climate change and science literacy. Place-based programs and visitor expectations for climate change communication were also evaluated through a National Science Foundation study conducted with Colorado State University, the National Parks Conservation Association, and the USFWS. Five workshops, 16 site visits, and a series of surveys with park staff and visitors were completed. Results reveal high public interest in receiving climate change science and adaptation information about protected areas and their resources. CALL TO ACTION ITEM 30: TOOLS OF THE TRADE

Communicating the Science of Sound: Natural Sounds staff and cooperators published 15 papers in peer-reviewed journals in FY 2011 and spearheaded social science research relative to wildlife and visitor responses to noise in several parks. The papers addressed an array of topics, from the effects of transportation systems on the acoustic environment to studies of visitor attitudes, norms, and beliefs concerning park soundscapes. The research expands understanding of how the acoustic environment affects wildlife and visitors to national parks and helps to ensure that management decisions are informed by peer-reviewed scientific data and analyses. Journals included *Landscape Ecology*, *Journal of Park and Recreation Administration*, *Human Dimensions of Wildlife*, *Journal of Transport Geography*, and others.

Critical Load Pilot Study: Air Quality program staff participated in the FOCUS (Focal Center United States) pilot study to link deposition and its effects on ecosystems in a quantitative, scientifically supportable manner. The project will enable a productive and meaningful dialogue with the international scientific community on methods for estimating, calculating, mapping, interpreting, and refining critical loads (the pollution loading at which sensitive systems are altered). This effort will permit the formulation and implementation of a strategic vision for developing and using critical loads for environmental policy, program assessment, and public land management in the United States.

Establishing a Natural Baseline for Night Skies: The Night Skies program has developed instrumentation that can precisely measure

Studying microbes on ceiling of Golden Dome Cave, Lava Beds National Monument, California
NPS/DALE PATE

the brightness of the night sky above national parks. Under fairly dark and unpolluted settings, however, natural features such as the Milky Way can obscure modest amounts of light pollution and confound the ability to track impacts on the night sky. A more accurate model of a natural night sky has been needed to isolate the percentage of overall night glow that can be attributed to light pollution. Staff captured an image of the night sky from Mauna Kea Observatory in Hawaii and analyzed the image to produce a much-improved model of the natural night sky. This allows staff to process the program's archive of night sky data to isolate just the artificial light. **CALL TO ACTION ITEM 27: STARRY, STARRY NIGHT**

Forest Health Pest Suppression Program: The Integrated Pest Management program reviews forest pest proposals and serves as a liaison with USFS field stations to promote NPS projects. Projects in 15 parks totaling $1,088,000 were funded in FY 2011 by USFS forest health pest suppression funds. These funds help manage two pests that threaten entire ecosystems—non-native hemlock wooly adelgid and native mountain pine beetle. Hemlock wooly adelgid projects were funded at **Black Canyon of the Gunnison National Park (CO); Blue Ridge Parkway (NC); Cumberland Gap National Historical Park (KY, TN, VA); Delaware Water Gap National Recreation Area (PA, NJ); New River Gorge National River (WV); Obed Wild and Scenic River (TN); Rocky Mountain National Park (CO);** and **Shenandoah National Park (VA)**. Douglas-fir and mountain pine beetle projects were undertaken at **Glacier National Park (MT); Grand Canyon National Park (AZ); Grand Teton National Park (WY); Great Basin National Park (NV); Great Smoky Mountains National Park (NC, TN);** and **Mount Rushmore National Memorial (SD)**. Dutch elm disease control and eradication projects were funded at National Capital Region parks.

Ocean and Coastal Park Guidance: To help the 85 ocean and coastal units in the National Park System better understand applicable laws, regulations, and policies, the Geologic Resources and Water Resources programs completed a reference manual during FY 2011. The manual provides a basic introduction to ocean and coastal jurisdictional concepts, vocabulary, authorities, and case studies. The manual facilitates the National Park Service's ability to work with other federal, state, and local agencies and stakeholders in addressing resource protection issues. In addition, the programs drafted a director's order and coastal sediment restoration guidance, both scheduled for publication in FY 2012.

Paleontological Resource Inventory and Monitoring: In FY 2011 Geologic Resources staff finished the paleontological resource inventory and monitoring report for the Central Alaska I&M Network, completing a 10-year effort to research and compile baseline paleontological resource data for all of the 32 I&M networks. As a result of this servicewide project, the number of parks with known fossil resources has expanded to 232. **CALL TO ACTION ITEM 28: PARK PULSE**

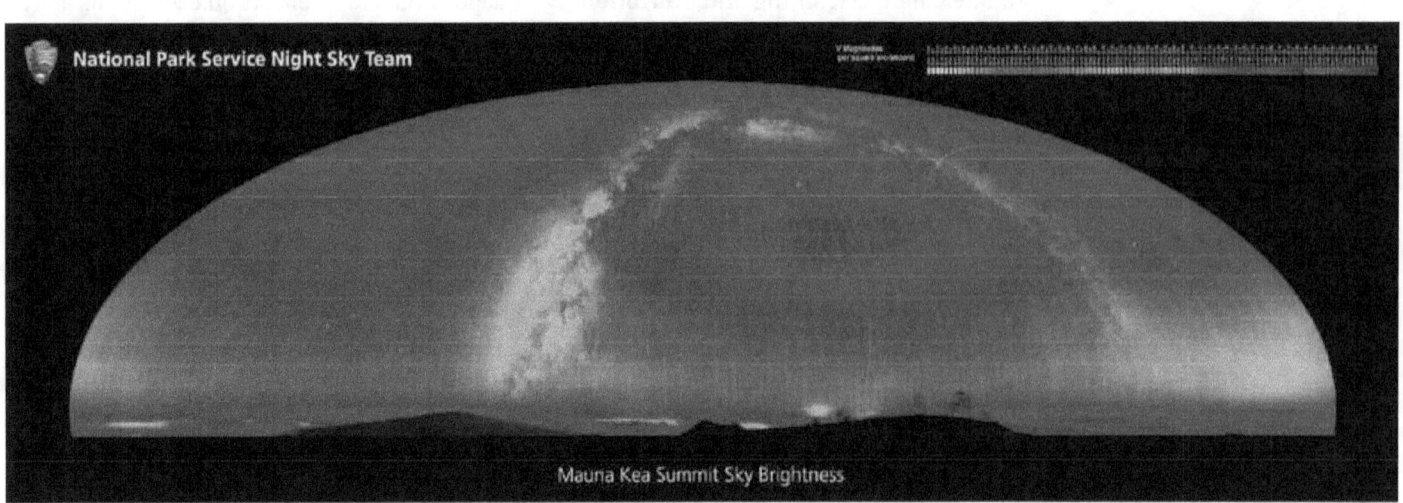

Sky brightness image from Mauna Kea Observatory showing Milky Way
NPS/DAN DURISCOE AND JEREMY WHITE

Sampling bees at Yellowstone National Park, Idaho, Montana, Wyoming
TOP: NPS PHOTO
BOTTOM: NPS/ANN RODMAN

Planning for Change: While some impacts from climate change are already measurable, the long-range effects of climate disruption on NPS natural and cultural resources, park infrastructure, and visitor experience are not well known. To cope with uncertainty, the National Park Service is implementing a scenario-based approach to planning that allows managers flexibility in using current science to incorporate strategic and tactical adaptation actions into long-range planning efforts. Four training workshops included more than 150 resource management, science, communication, and planning personnel. The workshops synthesized climate science and impacts for seven major bioregions (Great Lakes, Atlantic Coast, Eastern Forests, Urban Landscapes, Arid Lands, Pacific Islands, and Western Mountains) and explored adaptation actions and options for protecting natural and cultural resources and facilities.

Pollinator Response to Climate Change: Using simple and inexpensive collection methods, a pollinator response project is modeling the distribution of bee species in areas particularly vulnerable to climate change across the National Park System. The project represents both the largest accumulation of information on the distribution of pollinators and the largest geographic area over which such samples have been collected. Two hundred thirty-four samples were collected from 46 parks, resulting in the processing of nearly 8,000 bee specimens. Biodiversity was high, with 36 genera represented. Twenty-one Bombus (bumblebee) species were identified from ten parks, which is significant because many bumblebee species are declining around the world. In future years, this critical baseline information will allow managers to target species and habitats for future monitoring and restoration efforts. CALL TO ACTION ITEM 7: NEXT GENERATION STEWARDS

Power of Sound: The Natural Sounds and Night Skies program published the *Power of Sound Interpretive Handbook* to provide NPS interpreters with tools for developing programs that will connect visitors to park soundscapes and acoustic resources. The handbook acts as a reference for learning more about sound in NPS units and provides sample programs that can be adapted to meet a park's needs. The handbook helps further understanding of and public appreciation for the sounds of nature as well as cultural soundscapes. CALL TO ACTION ITEM 30: TOOLS OF THE TRADE

Renewable Energy: All servicewide natural resource programs participated in a renewable energy team, coordinated by the Geologic Resources program, that collaborated with other NPS directorates, federal agencies, and stakeholders to respond to and plan for increased renewable energy development on public lands. In FY 2011 the National Park Service became a cooperating agency under NEPA on dozens of renewable energy and electric transmission projects. NPS staff worked collaboratively with other DOI bureaus, including BLM, USFWS, Bureau of Indian Affairs, Bureau of Ocean Energy Management, and Bureau of Safety and Environmental Enforcement. They made significant contributions to renewable energy policies and guidance, including BLM guidance on processing solar and wind energy applications and USFWS wind energy guidelines. The National Park Service also instructed multi-agency staff on how to identify, avoid, and mitigate impacts to units of the National Park System. By contributing to the appropriate siting, design, and mitigation of renewable energy projects, the National Park Service is helping meet the Secretary of the Interior's renewable energy goals while fulfilling its obligation to protect parks from natural and cultural resource impacts.

Appendix A: Natural Resource Challenge Funding in Parks

Table A-1. Fiscal Year 2011 natural resource funding of National Park Service units receiving Natural Resource Challenge increases in FY 2001 or FY 2002

NPS unit	Fiscal year of Challenge funding increase	Amount of Challenge increase ($)	FY 2011 natural resource funding ($)
Acadia National Park	2002	345,000	831,308
Antietam National Battlefield	2001	150,000	427,500
Appalachian National Scenic Trail	2002	142,000	277,500
Big Cypress National Preserve	2001	399,000	1,236,500
Buck Island Reef National Monument	2001	100,000	216,000
Catoctin Mountain Park	2001	89,000	407,931
Channel Islands National Park	2002	498,000	2,479,877
Coronado National Memorial	2001	60,000	60,000
Curecanti National Recreation Area	2001	141,000	1,074,000
Dinosaur National Monument	2002	189,000	621,229
Gates of the Arctic National Park and Preserve	2002	148,000	496,159
Great Basin National Park	2002	126,000	537,725
Great Sand Dunes National Park and Preserve	2002	180,000	348,300
Great Smoky Mountains National Park	2001	402,000	2,478,847
Haleakala National Park	2001	480,000	1,495,371
Homestead National Monument of America	2002	82,000	112,237
Hopewell Culture National Historical Park	2002	105,000	100,714
Jewel Cave National Monument	2001	50,000	161,000
John Day Fossil Beds National Monument	2001	95,000	112,310
Kalaupapa National Historical Park	2002	211,000	549,000
Lake Clark National Park and Preserve	2002	147,000	285,000
Little River Canyon National Preserve	2002	85,000	138,547
Mojave National Preserve	2001	470,000	1,310,959
Monocacy National Battlefield	2002	118,000	116,000
Obed Wild and Scenic River	2002	195,000	185,207
Padre Island National Seashore	2002	95,000	1,680,241
Pictured Rocks National Lakeshore	2002	55,000	312,675
Rock Creek Park	2001	163,000	163,000
San Juan Island National Historical Park	2002	95,000	112,457
Saugus Iron Works National Historic Site	2001	58,000	58,000
Sequoia and Kings Canyon National Parks	2002	112,000	1,677,230
Stones River National Battlefield	2002	132,000	266,795
Sunset Crater, Walnut Canyon, & Wupatki National Monuments	2002	100,000	217,850
Theodore Roosevelt National Park	2001	133,000	390,785
Virgin Islands National Park	2001	399,000	399,000
Zion National Park	2001 / 2002	246,000	574,996
TOTAL		6,595,000	21,912,250

Student Conservation Association intern mapping invasive thickets in restored tallgrass prairie at Homestead National Monument of America, Nebraska
NPS/JESSE BOLLI

Appendix B: Natural Resource Program Funding–Servicewide Programs

Table B-1. FY 2011 funding for NPS natural resource programs

Program	Total available in FY 2010 ($)	Management efficiencies reduction[a] ($)	Base change ($)	Consolidated Changes[b] ($)	Total available in FY 2011 ($)	Change from FY 2010 ($)
Air Quality Program	8,884,000	-22,000		-20,000	8,842,000	-42,000
Biological Resource Management Program	9,969,000	-67,000		-23,000	9,879,000	-90,000
Climate Change Response Program[c]	10,000,000		-462,000	-23,000	9,515,000	-485,000
Cooperative Ecosystem Studies Units[d]	125,000				125,000	0
Geologic Resources Program	3,420,000	-16,000		-8,000	3,396,000	-24,000
Inventory and Monitoring Program[e]	45,495,000	-205,000	20,000	-105,000	45,205,000	-290,000
Natural Resource Data and Information Program	1,955,000	-13,000		-5,000	1,937,000	-18,000
Natural Resource Preservation Program	8,099,000			-19,000	8,080,000	-19,000
Natural Sounds Program	3,565,000	-14,000		-8,000	3,543,000	-22,000
Resource Damage Assessment and Restoration Program (incl. Oil Spill Pollution Act)	1,453,000	-6,000		-4,000	1,443,000	-10,000
Resource Protection Fund	283,000			-1,000	282,000	-1,000
Social Science Program	1,769,000	-9,000		-6,000	1,754,000	-15,000
Water Resources Program	13,870,000	-31,000		-32,000	13,807,000	-63,000

[a]Management efficiencies reduction reflects the directorate's prorated portion of the NPS share of Department of the Interior–wide cost savings resulting from strategic sourcing, travel, and IT consolidation savings.
[b]Consolidated changes includes program changes and an across-the-board cut.
[c]Base change includes transfer of a total of $462,000 to three regions to cover costs of CESU research coordinators to support the Climate Change Response Program.
[d]CESU funding listed here is for national network support; Table B-5 contains individual CESU funding.
[e]Base change reflects permanent transfer of funds from Olympic and North Cascades national parks back to the Inventory and Monitoring Program.

Table B-2. Air Quality Program funding by category, FY 2011

Category	FY 2011 funding ($)
Air quality monitoring, projects, and analysis	4,358,000
Collaboration and outreach	382,000
Program management and implementation	1,076,000
Technical assistance	3,026,000
TOTAL	8,842,000

Table B-3. Biological Resource Management Program funding by category, FY 2011

Category	FY 2011 funding ($)
Biological resource operations	515,400
Biological resource projects–national support	246,000
Development and new initiatives	188,000
Human dimension of biological resources	285,000
Restoration and adaptation	6,499,600
Wildlife conservation	885,000
Wildlife health	1,260,000
TOTAL	9,879,000

Table B-4. Climate Change Response Program funding by category, FY 2011

Category	FY 2011 funding ($)
Operations	1,500,000
Enhanced monitoring	2,994,600
Adaptation	5,482,400
TOTAL [a]	9,977,000

[a]Total includes $462,000 that was transferred to three regions to cover costs of CESU research coordinators to support the Climate Change Response Program.

Table B-5 Allocation of funding among Cooperative Ecosystem Studies Units, FY 2011

Unit	Fiscal year first funded	FY 2011 funding ($)
Californian[a]	2010	154,000
Chesapeake Watershed	2001	155,000
Colorado Plateau	2001	155,000
Desert Southwest	2001	155,000
Great Basin	2001	155,000
Great Lakes-Northern Forest	2003	155,000
Great Plains	2001	155,000
Great Rivers[a]	2010	154,000
Gulf Coast	2003	155,000
Hawaii-Pacific Islands[a,b]		
North and West Alaska[a]	2010	154,000
North Atlantic Coast	2001	155,000
Pacific Northwest	2001	155,000
Piedmont-South Atlantic Coast[a,b]		
Rocky Mountains	2001	155,000
South Florida-Caribbean	2001	155,000
Southern Appalachian Mountains	2001	155,000
TOTAL		2,322,000

[a]These CESUs were not funded by the Natural Resource Challenge.
[b]NPS regional offices support these CESUs through funding, collateral duties of regional office staff, and/or assignment of duties to coordinators of other CESU networks.

Table B-6. Geologic Resources Program funding by category, FY 2011

Category	FY 2011 funding ($)
Cave and karst management	180,800
Coastal geology and engineering	463,900
Disturbed lands restoration/abandoned mineral lands	324,600
External renewable energy coordination	291,300
Geologic hazards mitigation	36,200
Geologic heritage resources	97,300
Geologic resources inventory and assessment	129,000
Geoscientists-in-the-Parks	451,000
Mining and minerals management	81,600
National Cave and Karst Research Institute	323,000
Oil and gas management	398,800
Program support	220,000
Paleontological resources management	197,300
Soil resources management	157,600
Upland and fluvial processes	43,600
TOTAL	3,396,000

Table B-7. Inventory and Monitoring Program funding by category, FY 2011

Category	FY 2011 funding ($)
Information management	888,108
Natural resource inventories	11,007,857
Operations	1,525,498
Regional program managers	1,023,400
Vital signs monitoring	30,760,137
TOTAL[a]	45,205,000

[a]Total funding reflects permanent transfer of funds from Olympic and North Cascades national parks back to Inventory and Monitoring Program.

Table B-8. Allocation of funding among basic natural resource inventories, FY 2011

Category	FY 2011 funding ($)
Air quality data	90,000
Alaska vegetation and soil inventories	1,000,000
Dark night skies inventories	128,000
Geologic resources inventories	1,925,000
Soil resources inventories	2,500,000
Submerged resources inventories	300,000
Vegetation inventories	4,175,549
Other natural resource inventories	889,308
TOTAL	11,007,857

Table B-9. Allocation of monitoring funding among Inventory and Monitoring Networks, FY 2011

Network[a]	Fiscal year first funded	Number of parks in network	Water quality monitoring ($)	Vital signs monitoring ($)
Alaska Region				
Arctic	2005	5	144,100	1,631,000
Central Alaska	2002	3	94,200	1,303,300
Southeast Alaska	2006	3	40,400	505,000
Southwest Alaska	2002	5	133,600	1,513,300
Intermountain Region				
Chihuahuan Desert	2007	6	70,200	804,000
Greater Yellowstone	2002	3	68,200	780,000
Northern Colorado Plateau	2002	16	103,700	1,072,000
Rocky Mountain	2004	6	58,600	677,000
Sonoran Desert	2001	11	61,500	733,000
Southern Colorado Plateau	2003	19	119,100	1,286,000
Southern Plains	2006	10	27,900	480,000
Midwest Region				
Great Lakes	2003	9	118,200	1,402,000
Heartland	2001	15	78,800	825,500
Northern Great Plains	2007	13	77,900	967,000
National Capital Region				
National Capital	2002	11	68,200	815,100
Northeast Region				
Eastern Rivers and Mountains	2004	9	60,600	678,300
Mid-Atlantic	2006	10	42,300	377,500
Northeast Coastal and Barrier	2001	8	86,500	802,000
Northeast Temperate	2003	11	57,700	832,000
Pacific West Region				
Klamath	2004	6	73,000	850,000
Mediterranean Coast	2002	3	73,000	400,000
Mojave Desert	2006	6	76,900	925,400
North Coast and Cascades	2001	7	78,800	1,258,000
Pacific Island	2003	9	145,100	1,627,100
San Francisco Bay Area	2002	6	67,200	825,000
Sierra Nevada	2004	3	60,600	700,000
Upper Columbia Basin	2006	8	48,000	566,500
Southeast Region				
Appalachian Highlands	2002	4	67,200	465,000
Cumberland/Piedmont	2001	14	56,700	1,023,300
Gulf Coast	2004	8	85,500	977,000
South Florida/Caribbean	2006	6	141,300	1,610,500
Southeast Coast	2005	17	116,300	1,340,400
Service-wide Data Management			136,600	
TOTAL[b]		270	2,737,900	30,052,200

[a] Networks are listed by the region that includes the majority of the network area, even though the network may extend into other regions.
[b] Vital signs monitoring funding in this table does not include national program costs; the total, therefore, differs from Table B-7.

Table B-10. Natural Sounds and Night Skies Program funding by categories, FY 2011

Category	FY 2011 funding ($)
Acoustic inventories	114,188
Air tour management support	950,000
Technical assistance	2,478,812
TOTAL	3,543,000

Table B-11. Water Resources Program funding by categories, FY 2011

Category	FY 2011 funding ($)
Natural resource condition assessments	2,335,700
Ocean and coastal resources	965,000
Water quality vital signs monitoring	2,737,900
Water resource projects	1,166,900
Water resource protection-aquatic resource professionals	1,327,400
Water resource technical assistance	5,274,100
TOTAL	13,807,000

Appendix C: Biological Resource Management Competitive Projects

Table C-1. Biological resource projects, FY 2011

Region	State	Park	Project title	FY 2011 funding ($)
AKR	AK	Denali National Park and Preserve	Assessing the impacts of climate change on at-risk boreal forest wetland nesting birds in Denali NP&P	22,000
		Katmai National Park and Preserve	Measuring abundance of kokanee in Katmai NP&P	25,000
IMR	AZ	Saguaro National Park	Test effectiveness of different control methods on invasive buffelgrass	25,000
	CO	Black Canyon of the Gunnison National Park	Restoring Gunnison grouse habitat as part of Crawford population recovery effort	16,000
	NM	Carlsbad Caverns National Park	Determine biodiversity patterns of native bee pollinators in the Chihuahuan Desert of Carlsbad Caverns	25,000
	TX	Guadalupe Mountains National Park	Create experimental colony(ies) of imperiled species of endemic Guadalupe Mountains violet	25,000
	TX	Padre Island National Seashore	Assess impacts of beach recreational activities on endangered shorebirds	17,000
MWR	MI	Isle Royale National Park	Ecological factors affecting extreme genetic and phenotypic diversity in Lake Trout at Isle Royale NP	25,000
	MI	Pictured Rocks National Lakeshore	Assess interactions of Unionid mussels, yellow perch, and lake trout in Grand Sable Lake at Pictured Rocks NL	23,000
PWR	WA	Mount Rainier National Park	Protect rare bat colonies	25,000
SER	SC	Congaree National Park	Evaluate dormant season herbicide treatment methods for Chinese privet at Congaree NP	18,000
TOTAL				246,000

Appendix D: Climate Change Response Program Projects

Table D-1. Climate Change Response projects, FY 2011

Region	State	Landscape Conservation Cooperative	Park	Project title	FY 2011 funding ($) Project funds	FY 2011 funding ($) Program funds
AKR	AK	North Pacific, Western Alaska, Aleutian and Bering Sea Islands, Arctic, Northwestern Interior Forest	Alaska Regional Office	Climate change scenario planning for national parks in Alaska	100,000	75,000
	MT	Great Northern	Glacier National Park	Ice patches as sources of archeological and paleoecological data in climate change research	150,000	100,000
	TX	Gulf Coast Plains and Ozarks	Big Thicket National Preserve	Develop freshwater flow recommendations to mitigate effects of climate change to estuarine habitats	0	92,000
MWR	Multiple	Upper Midwest and Great Lakes	Indiana Dunes National Seashore	Determine the effects of changing climate on the demography of the Karner blue butterfly	137,000	73,000
	SD	Plains and Prairie Potholes	Wind Cave National Park	Quantitative forecasting of above and below ground climate change impacts at Wind Cave	176,000	42,000
NCR	Multiple	North Atlantic	National Capital Regional Office	Modeling coastal vulnerability for freshwater tidal reaches of the Potomac and Anacostia rivers	141,000	49,000
NER	ME	North Atlantic	Acadia National Park	Inventory and protect salt marshes from risks of sea level rise at Acadia NP, Maine	65,000	30,000
	VA	Appalachian	Shenandoah National Park	Adaptive management, climate change, and endangered species: A case study of Shenandoah salamanders	124,000	94,000
PWR	CA	California	Pacific West Regional Office, Golden Gate National Recreation Area, Sequoia and Kings Canyon National Parks, Lassen Volcanic National Park, Redwood National and State Parks, Joshua Tree National Park, Santa Monica Mountains National Recreation Area	Facilitate phenology network to assess climate change response in California parks	106,000	96,000
	CA	California	Yosemite National Park	Impacts of fire management on carbon stock stability in Yosemite, Sequoia, and Kings Canyon NPs	172,000	0
	WA	North Pacific	Olympic National Park	Response of Olympic glaciers to climate change	37,000	0
SER	FL	n/a	Southeast Archeological Center	Climate change response, adaptation and NHL documentation for prehistoric mound sites	0	88,000
	FL, MS	Gulf Coastal Plains and Ozarks	Gulf Islands National Seashore	Endangered beach mouse: Linking population studies/habitat restoration to predicted sea level rise	25,000	0
	SC	South Atlantic	Congaree National Park	Climate change-induced changes in flow regime, floodplain inundation and species habitats at Congaree	131,000	35,000
Multiple	Multiple	Every LCC except Pacific Islands, and Peninsular Florida	Yellowstone National Park (lead—75 parks involved)	Multi-regional evaluation of pollinator response to climate change in critical habitats servicewide	152,000	90,000

Table D-1 (cont). Climate Change Response projects, FY 2011

Region	State	Landscape Conservation Cooperative	Park	Project title	FY 2011 funding ($) Project funds	FY 2011 funding ($) Program funds
	Multiple	Great Basin, Southern Rockies, North Pacific	Lassen Volcanic National Park, Rocky Mountain National Park, Great Sand Dunes National Park and Preserve, Grand Teton National Park, Yellowstone National Park, Lava Beds National Monument, Crater Lake National Park, Craters of the Moon National Monument and Preserve	Pikas in peril: Multi-regional vulnerability assessment of a climate-sensitive sentinel species	180,000	76,000
	Multiple	Northern Rockies, Southern Rockies	Rocky Mountain National Park, Grand Teton National Park, Yellowstone National Park, Great Sand Dunes National Park and Preserve	A cooperative plan for wolverine recovery and management in the conterminous U.S.	96,000	0
	Multiple	South Rockies, Desert, Great Basin	Mojave National Preserve, Grand Canyon National Park, Glen Canyon National Recreation Area, Lake Mead National Recreation Area, Capitol Reef National Park, Canyonlands National Park, Arches National Park, Zion National Park	Assessing climate refugia and connectivity for desert bighorn sheep	$8,000	27,000
TOTAL					1,800,000	967,000

Table D-2. George Melendez Wright Climate Change Fellowship projects, FY 2011

Region	State	Landscape Conservation Cooperative	Park	Project title	FY 2011 program funds ($)
AKR	AK	North Pacific	Glacier Bay National Park and Preserve	Understanding human and ecological responses to yellow-cedar decline in southeast Alaska's coastal rainforests: A case study looking at what climate-related changes in forest communities mean for conservation and management planning	19,179
AKR/IMR/PWR	Multiple	North Pacific, Great Northern, California	Glacier Bay National Park and Preserve, Yellowstone National Park, Yosemite National Park	Discrete populations? Examining the role of genetic variation and landscape heterogeneity in the phenotypic divergence of Pinus contorta	19,200
IMR	CO	Southern Rockies	Rocky Mountain National Park	Linking climate drivers to the timing of willow (Salix spp.) decline in Rocky Mountain NP	19,684
	CO	Southern Rockies	Mesa Verde National Park	The effects of fire and fire management practices on mercury fate and transport in Mesa Verde NP	20,000
	MT	Great Northern	Glacier National Park	Investigating how climate induced changes in alpine glaciers alter phytoplankton communities and lake habitat	12,372
MWR	MI	Upper Midwest and Great Lakes	Sleeping Bear Dunes National Lakeshore	How do microbial symbioses affect plant community and ecosystem responses to climate change? A test in the dunes of Sleeping Bear Dunes NL	19,965
NER	ME	North Atlantic	Acadia National Park	Reconstructing past plant phenology in Acadia NP: Tracking climate change through herbarium specimens, written records, and historic photographs	12,004
PWR	Multiple	Pacific Islands	Kaloko-Honokōhau National Historical Park, Kalaupapa National Historical Park, Haleakala National Park, Hawaii Volcanoes National Park, National Park of American Samoa	Coral resilience and resistance in the National Parks of the Pacific Islands during times of global change	18,617
	CA	California	Channel Islands National Park	Assessment of ocean acidification in the Channel Islands National Park and its impact on local marine species	19,987
	WA	North Pacific	Olympic National Park	Harmful algal blooms and climate in Olympic NP	18,908
SER	FL	Peninsular Florida	Everglades National Park	Detecting long-term community shifts in response to sea level rise and Everglades' restoration: Can remote sensing, competitive ability, and life stage be used in guiding conservation actions?	20,000
TOTAL					199,915

Table D-3. George Melendez Wright Climate Change Internship projects, FY 2011

Region	State	Landscape Conservation Cooperative	Park	Project Title	FY 2011 program funds ($)
IMR	CO	Southern Rockies	Rocky Mountain National Park	Measuring nitrogen and CO2 flux in tundra soils and developing public educational materials about greenhouse gases in the park	9,338
	MT	Great Northern	Glacier National Park	Research on climate change impacts on mountain goats and pikas	9,338
IMR/PWR	Multiple	Great Northern	Great Northern LCC	Assisting with establishment of an LCC	10,886
MWR	Multiple	Great Northern	Lewis and Clark National Historic Trail	Helping plan and develop a plant phenology citizen science project as part of a national program	9,338
	OH	Upper Midwest and Great Lakes	Cuyahoga Valley National Park	Developing products to educate school groups and the general public about climate change	9,338
	WI	Upper Midwest and Great Lakes	Apostle Islands National Lakeshore	Understanding climate change impacts through science and traditional Ojibwe knowledge	9,338
NCR	DC	North Atlantic	Center for Urban Ecology	Planning and development of a plant phenology citizen science program	10,807
NER	MA	North Atlantic	Cape Cod National Seashore	Developing public programs and interpretive materials on coastal impacts of climate change	9,338
PWR	CA	California	Santa Monica Mountains National Recreation Area	Developing field-based climate change lesson plans for elementary and middle school groups	9,338
	CA	Desert	Death Valley National Park	Development of science-based climate change lesson plans for rural and urban school groups	9,338
	OR	Great Northern	John Day Fossil Beds National Monument	Developing products to educate the public about past climate change and lessons for current and future change	9,338
	WA	North Pacific	North Cascades National Park	Documenting and teaching youth about improvements in sustainability of park operations	9,338
SER	LA	Gulf Coast Prairie	Jean Lafitte National Historical Park and Preserve	Research on effects of canal removal and sea level rise on coastal wetland ecology	9,338
WASO	DC	n/a	Office of Public Health	Statistical modelling to predict where and when people are at risk of tick-borne diseases under future climate change	9,338
TOTAL					133,750

Table D-4. Additional projects funded by the Climate Change Response Program, FY 2011

Region	State	Landscape Conservation Cooperative	Park	Project Title	FY 2011 program funds ($)
All	All	All	All	Climate change interpretive training and curriculum development	30,000
All	All	All	All	Climate change scenario planning for the NPS	120,000
All	All	All	All	Multi-agency, NGO adaptation guidebook	50,000
All	All	All	All	NPS Climate Change Action Plan	324,520
IMR	ND	Plains and Prairie Potholes	Theodore Roosevelt National Park	Climate change, river flow, and riparian cottonwood forests	68,088
TOTAL					592,608

Appendix E: Natural Sounds Projects

Table E-1. Natural sounds projects, FY 2011

Region	State	Parks	Project title	FY 2011 funding ($)
IMR	UT	Zion National Park	Collect soundscape data for air tour management plan – phase 2	34,000
PWR	CA	Golden Gate National Recreation Area	Prepare air tour management plan for San Francisco Bay Area parks	33,000
	HI	Haleakala National Park	Complete Haleakala air tour management plan	59,000
	HI	Hawaii Volcanoes National Park	Complete Hawaii Volcanoes air tour management plan	41,000
	OR	Crater Lake National Park	Measure acoustical baseline at Crater Lake NP in advance of air tour management planning	38,000
	WA	Mount Rainier National Park	Characterize acoustic conditions for soundscape management planning	38,000
	WA	Olympic National Park	Characterize the soundscape of a large wilderness park	26,000
TOTAL				269,000

Appendix F: Water Resource Program Projects

Table F-1. National Park Service sites with natural resource condition assessment projects in FY 2011 and organization performing the assessments

Region	State	Parks	Agency, cooperator/partner, or contractor	FY 2011 funding ($)
AKR	AK	Katmai National Park, Aniakchak National Monument and Preserve, Alagnak Wild River	Pacific Northwest CESU/Saint Mary's University of Minnesota	101,000
	Multiple	Multiple	Regional office project support	60,300
IMR	CO, MT, OK	Little Bighorn Battlefield National Monument, Sand Creek Massacre National Historic Site, Washita Battlefield National Historic Site	Rocky Mountain CESU/Utah State University, University of Colorado, Colorado State University, NPS Southern Plains Inventory & Monitoring Network, NPS Rocky Mountain Inventory & Monitoring Network	60,056
	CO, NM, CO	Bandelier National Monument, Black Canyon of the Gunnison National Park, Curecanti National Recreation Area, Petroglyph National Monument, Zion National Park	U.S. Geological Survey Fort Collins Science Center, Colorado Plateau CESU/Museum of Northern Arizona, NPS Northern Colorado and Southern Colorado Plateau Networks	167,000
	MT, WY	Bighorn Canyon National Recreation Area	Pacific Northwest CESU/Saint Mary's University of Minnesota, NPS Greater Yellowstone Inventory & Monitoring Network	38,700
	TX	Big Bend National Park, Guadalupe Mountains National Park	Pacific Northwest CESU/Saint Mary's University of Minnesota	115,000
	TX	Padre Island National Seashore, Palo Alto Battlefield National Historic Site	Pacific Northwest CESU/Saint Mary's University of Minnesota	15,000
	Multiple	Multiple	Regional office Geographic Information Systems (GIS) and other project support	67,544
MWR	MN, WI	Grand Portage National Monument, Mississippi National River & Recreation Area, Saint Croix National Scenic Riverway, Voyageurs National Park	Great Lakes Northern Forest CESU/ University of Wisconsin-Stevens Point	302,000
NCR	DC, MD, WV	Catoctin Mountain Park, Chesapeake and Ohio Canal National Historical Park (upper portion)	Chesapeake Watershed CESU/ University of Maryland, NPS National Capital Inventory & Monitoring Network	74,000
	Multiple	Multiple	Regional office project support	6,700
NER	Multiple	Multiple	Regional office project support	100,902
	VA	Booker T Washington National Monument, Petersburg National Battlefield	Chesapeake Watershed CESU/ University of Richmond	84,962
	VA	Fredericksburg & Spotsylvania National Military Park	Chesapeake Watershed CESU/ Pennsylvania State University	56,136
PWR	AZ, CA, NV,	Death Valley National Park, Joshua Tree National Park, Lake Mead National Recreation Area, Manzanar National Historic Site, Mojave National Preserve, Grand Canyon-Parashant National Monument	Californian CESU, University of California-Davis	275,000
PWR	CA	Yosemite National Park	Yosemite National Park	20,000
	CA, OR	Crater Lake National Park, Lassen Volcanic National Park, Lava Beds National Monument	Pacific Northwest CESU/ Southern Oregon University	25,000
	HI	Hawaii Volcanoes National Park	Fung Associates	42,250
	Multiple	Multiple	Regional office project support	6,450
	WA	Mount Rainier National Park, North Cascades National Park	U.S. Geological Survey-Forest and Rangelands Ecosystem Center	75,000

Table F-1 (cont). National Park Service sites with natural resource condition assessment projects in FY 2011 and organization performing the assessments

Region	State	Parks	Agency, cooperator/partner, or contractor	FY 2011 funding ($)
SER	AL, FL, GA, NC, SC	Cape Hatteras National Seashore, Cape Lookout National Seashore, Chattahoochee River National Recreation Area, Congaree National Park, Cumberland Island National Seashore, Horseshoe Bend National Military Park, Kennesaw Mountain National Battlefield Park, Moores Creek National Battlefield, Ocmulgee National Monument, Timucuan Ecological and Historic Preserve	Piedmont-South Atlantic Coast CESU/North Carolina State University	92,122
	FL	Big Cypress National Preserve, Everglades National Park	NPS South Florida/Caribbean I&M Network	26,678
	Multiple	Multiple	Regional office project support	80,900
	NC	Carl Sandburg Home National Historic Site	Southern Appalachian CESU/ University of Western Carolina	123,000
TOTAL				2,015,700

Table F-2. Natural Resource Condition Assessment high-priority water resource project funding, FY 2011

Region	State	Park	Project title	FY 2011 funding ($)
IMR	CO, UT	Dinosaur National Monument	Evaluation of Yampa River flow and sediment regimes to assist protection of river-dependent resource attributes	75,000
PWR	CA	Yosemite National Park	Wawona Meadow wetland restoration storm repair request	53,000
	HI	Kaloko-Honokōhau National Historical Park	Develop an environmental assessment and eradication plan to remove tilapia from ponds and wetlands at national parks on Hawai'i Island: Aimakapa Pond Wetland at Kaloko-Honokōhau NHP and other sites of concern	63,000
	ID	Nez Perce National Historical Park	Hydrological analysis and pilot restoration project for Weippe Prairie, Nez Perce NHP, Idaho	26,200
Service-wide	Multiple	Multiple	EarthSoft environmental quality information system acquisition	96,650
	Multiple	Multiple	General project support	6,150
TOTAL				320,000

Table F-3. Water resource protection projects, FY 2011

Region	State	Park	Project title	FY 2011 funding ($)
IMR	CO, UT	Dinosaur National Monument	Hydrologic data collection for Green and Yampa rivers	93,120
	NM	White Sands National Monument	Hydrologic data collection for Tularosa Aquifer	75,000
	SD	Wind Cave National Park	Lab analyses for cave evolution study	15,000
	TX	Big Bend National Park	Determination of outstandingly remarkable values	28,000
	TX	Big Bend National Park	Hydrologic data collection for the Rio Grande	20,000
	WY	Grand Teton National Park	Engineering services for water right change application on Spread Creek	2,500
PWR	AZ, NV	Lake Mead National Recreation Area	Hydrologic data collection on Virgin River	5,400
	CA	Death Valley National Park	Hydrologic data analysis for Devils Hole	30,800
	HI	Kaloko-Honokōhau National Historical Park	Investigation of hydrology and water dependent values	78,800
	NV	Great Basin National Park	Investigation of hydrogeology and hydrologic data collection	46,600
Service-wide	Multiple	Multiple	Support to the Office of the Solicitor to protect/secure NPS water resources	192,750
	Multiple	Multiple	Support to the U.S. Geological Survey to process hydrologic data	23,760
	Multiple	Multiple	Technical support and assistance for all projects	46,900
TOTAL				658,630

Table F-4. Ocean and coastal resource project funding, FY 2011

Region	State	Park	Project title	FY 2011 funding ($)
AKR	AK	Multiple (10)	Compilation of an accurate and contemporary digital shoreline for Alaska coastal parks	21,000
NER	MA	Cape Cod National Seashore	Investigations of the linkages between toxic red tides, hydrodynamics, and groundwater nutrient fluxes at Cape Cod NS	92,000
PWR	CA	Channel Islands National Park	Marine benthic habitat mapping of Channel Islands NP	299,950
	HI	Kaloko-Honokōhau National Historical Park and Kalaupapa National Historical Park	Managing marine ecosystem responses to increasing nutrients	83,000
SER	USVI	Virgin Islands Coral Reef National Monument and Virgin Islands National Park	Ecological linkages between Virgin Islands Coral Reef NM and Virgin Islands NP: Management to halt the crisis of low reef fish populations	37,000
Service-wide	Multiple	Multiple (84)	Legal and regulatory assistance on ocean and coastal issues faced by the National Park System	52,000
TOTAL				584,950

Table F-5. Legacy high priority project funding, FY 2011

Region	State	Park	Project title	FY 2011 funding ($)
MWR	ND	Theodore Roosevelt National Park	Flow diversion, drought stress, and cottonwood sex ratios at Theodore Roosevelt NP	13,700
	SD	Wind Cave National Park	Black Hills area groundwater flow model	15,000
PWR	CA	Channel Islands National Park	Prisoner's Harbor supplemental plant propagation	40,000
	CA	Golden Gate National Recreation Area	Install water level recorders	9,950
Service-wide	Multiple	Multiple	Cooperative Fisheries Program	14,250
	Multiple	Multiple	Dive Safety Program	50,000
	Multiple	Multiple	Water quality partnership investigations	79,600
TOTAL				222,500

Appendix G: Resource Protection (RP) Projects

Table G-1. Resource Protection projects, FY 2011

Region	State	Park	Project title	FY 2011 funding ($)
AKR	AK	Glacier Bay National Park and Preserve	Protect bears from human caused mortalities, disturbance, and displacement	15,000
IMR	AZ	Petrified Forest National Park	Inventory and protect critical natural resources on expansion lands	38,800
MWR	AR	Buffalo National River	Protecting poached plant communities	25,000
	MI	Pictured Rocks National Lakeshore	Address illegal off-road vehicle use and restore damaged areas at Pictured Rocks NL	49,700
	MI	Sleeping Bear Dunes National Lakeshore	North Manitou wilderness restoration and protection	46,700
PWR	CA	Whiskeytown National Recreation Area	Develop best management practices to confront marijuana cultivation in parks	69,800
SER	NC, TN	Great Smoky Mountains National Park	Establish proactive aversive conditioning training program to protect wildlife and visitors	25,000
	KY	Mammoth Cave National Park	Protecting and preserving poached plant communities	12,000
TOTAL				282,000

Appendix H: Natural Resource Preservation Program (NRPP) Projects

Table H-1. NRPP–Alaska Special Projects, FY 2011

Park	Project title	FY 2011 funding ($)
Denali National Park and Preserve	Studying the movements and demography of road corridor bears in Denali NP	23,812
Denali National Park and Preserve	Create an ecological atlas of central Alaska's flora for management, research, and education	25,726
Denali National Park and Preserve	Design and test survey techniques to estimate Dall's sheep abundance in Alaskan parks	22,413
Denali National Park and Preserve	Assess threats to Denali NP&P's class I airshed through comprehensive analysis of long-term data	57,242
Glacier Bay National Park and Preserve	Implementing DIDSON sonar for assessing salmon escapement in Alaska national park wilderness	94,277
Kenai Fjords National Park	Upgrade Exit Glacier cooperative weather station to automated SNOTEL station	28,884
Western Arctic National Parklands	Non-invasive black bear population metrics in Kobuk Valley NP	71,389
Wrangell-St. Elias National Park and Preserve	Burbot stock assessment in Tanada Lake and Copper Lake in Wrangell-St. Elias NP&P	45,444
Wrangell-St. Elias National Park and Preserve	Continuing research on the occurrence and distribution of coastal and anadromous fish in Wrangell-St. Elias NP&P	12,117
Wrangell-St. Elias National Park and Preserve	Improve subsistence management with current information on resource use by Copper Basin communities	70,784
Lake Clark National Park and Preserve	Assess wolf population status and predation rate in Lake Clark NP&P	10,242
Other		4,670
TOTAL		467,000

Table H-2. NRPP–Disturbed Lands Restoration projects, FY 2011

Region	State	Park	Project title	FY 2011 funding ($)
IMR	AZ	Grand Canyon National Park	Restore disturbed habitat of threatened and endangered sentry milk-vetch, a Grand Canyon endemic	17,820
	MT	Glacier National Park	Stabilization of eroding soils and restoration of vegetation to the Big Bend Area, Glacier NP	9,900
	WY	Grand Teton National Park	Restore ecological processes and native vegetation to the former Flagg Ranch site	125,730
MWR	AR	Buffalo National River	Stabilization of extreme bank erosion to protect rare native mussel beds at Buffalo NR	87,120
NER	MD, VA	Assateague Island National Seashore	Restore salt marsh ecosystem function by removing relict mosquito ditches	99,000
PWR	CA	Channel Islands National Park	Restore disturbed coastal wetlands at Prisoners Harbor, Santa Cruz Island	165,000
	CA	Golden Gate National Recreation Area	From parking lot to wetland: Habitat restoration within the Rodeo Lagoon Watershed	120,000
	CA	Sequoia and Kings Canyon National Parks	Restore critical wetlands in Lower Halstead Meadow crossed by the primary park Generals Highway	77,000
	CA	Whiskeytown National Recreation Area	Restore geomorphology of Paige-Boulder Watershed to reestablish habitat for T&E species	86,000
Other				2,430
TOTAL				790,000

Table H-3. NRPP–Natural Resource Management projects, FY 2011

Region	State	Park	Project title	FY 2011 funding ($)
AKR	AK	Glacier Bay National Park and Preserve	Determine impacts of increased cruise ship traffic on endangered humpback whales	2,970
	AK	Kenai Fjords National Park	Understanding spatio-temporal variability within colonial nesting seabird populations	91,080
	AK	Wrangell-St. Elias National Park and Preserve	Understanding population declines of Kittlitz's murrelet in Icy Bay, Wrangell-St. Elias NP&P	116,820
IMR	AZ	Organ Pipe Cactus National Monument	Illegal migration in AZ border parks: Assessment, protection, and restoration of resources	99,000
	AZ	Saguaro National Park	Restore native saguaro community following removal of invasives	64,350
	MT, WY	Bighorn Canyon National Recreation Area	Arid land spring protection and restoration	42,570
	NM	Bandelier National Monument	Restore degraded pinon-juniper landscape: Phase I (of 3)	127,710
	TX	Amistad National Recreation Area	Survey and monument 34.5 miles of impacted park boundary	38,610
	TX	Big Bend National Park	Reconnaissance of water chemistry and spring flow from a trans-border aquifer along the Rio Grande	69,300
	WY	Grand Teton National Park	Native plant restoration of critical wildlife habitat	130,680
MWR	MI	Sleeping Bear Dunes National Lakeshore	Identify the sources, species & pathways in recent Type E botulism waterfowl dieoffs within Sleeping Bear Dunes NL	29,700
	ND	Theodore Roosevelt National Park	Development of an elk survey protocol for Theodore Roosevelt NP	102,960
	SD	Badlands National Park	Determine erosion rates at select fossil sites to develop a paleontological monitoring program	102,960
	SD	Wind Cave National Park	Evaluate elk population control and support adaptive management at Wind Cave NP	83,160
NCR	DC, MD, WV	Chesapeake and Ohio Canal National Historical Park	Assessing the vulnerability of sensitive karst habitats containing RTE species in Chesapeake and Ohio Canal NHP	100,000
	Multiple	National Capital Regional Office	Detecting and mapping new invasive species occurrences	17,000
NER	NY	Fire Island National Seashore	Assessment of spawning horseshoe crabs within mid-Atlantic coastal NPS units	84,000
	NY	Fire Island National Seashore	Restoration of bayside sediment processes at Sailors Haven, Fire Island NS	131,000
	WV	New River Gorge National River	Inventory and assess cliff resources and visitor use, develop cliff management & monitoring plan	71,280
PWR	Amer. Samoa	National Park of American Samoa	Eliminate a pivotal invasive tree species from National Park of American Samoa	99,000
	CA	Channel Islands National Park	Eradicate alien Argentine ants on Santa Cruz Island, Channel Islands NP	57,000
	CA	Channel Islands National Park	Eradicate iceplant and restore native vegetation on Anacapa Island	137,000
	CA	Pinnacles National Monument	Get the lead out: Gain support for non-lead hunting practices	99,000
	CA	Pinnacles National Monument	Protect recently acquired sensitive new lands from exotic pigs	35,000
	CA	Pinnacles National Monument	Restore rare bottomlands of newly acquired ranch	52,000

Table H-3 (cont). NRPP–Natural Resource Management projects, FY 2011

Region	State	Park	Project title	FY 2011 funding ($)
	CA	Point Reyes National Seashore	Marine resource assessment for marine protected areas	60,000
	CA	Point Reyes National Seashore	Stop Scotch broom invasion into wilderness and high-priority areas	103,000
	CA	Santa Monica Mountains National Recreation Area	Sources, prevalence, and impacts of anticoagulant poisons on wildlife in an urban national park	80,000
	HI	Haleakala National Park	Control ecosystem-modifying weeds and initiate restoration of the newly acquired Nuu addition, Haleakala NP	67,000
	WA	Olympic National Park	Identify potential barriers, corridors, and refugia for species in the face of climate change	72,000
	WA	Olympic National Park	Understanding trends of sport fishing on critical fishery resources in Olympic NP rivers and lakes	73,000
SER	FL	Dry Tortugas National Park	Dry Tortugas Research Natural Area implementation	94,000
	GA	Cumberland Island National Seashore	Spatial and temporal assessment of back-barrier erosion on Cumberland Island	64,123
	KY	Mammoth Cave National Park	Environmental modeling and management to restore air flow and protect cave resources in Mammoth Cave	96,677
	KY, TN	Big South Fork National River and Recreation Area	Develop a GIS model to predict information critical for development of Big South Fork's climbing management plan	50,312
	NC	Blue Ridge Parkway	Develop wetlands management plan and establish baseline data on Blue Ridge Parkway wetlands	79,907
	NC, TN	Great Smoky Mountains National Park	Preserving Smoky Mountain hemlock forests from destruction by an invasive insect	115,421
	TN	Stones River National Battlefield	Exploratory hydrology of limestone glades	38,493
Service-wide	Multiple	Multiple	Complete night sky assessments in class I parks and initiate monitoring	155,000
Other				17,918
TOTAL[a,b]				3,151,000

[a]The total reflects $12,000 reallocated between the Golden Gate NRA and Pinnacles NM projects funded through Threatened and Endangered Species and the Point Reyes NS Scotch broom project funded through Natural Resource Management.
[b]$22,500 in NRPP funds were reallocated from Natural Resource Management to Servicewide projects to complete their obligation at the close of FY 2011.

Table H-4. NRPP–Regional Program Block Allocation projects, FY 2011

Region	State	Park	Project title	FY 2011 funding ($)
AKR	AK	Alaska Regional Office	Alaska scientific and technical reports	5,940
	AK	Alaska Regional Office	Manage invasive weeds using herbicides in 9 Alaska Region parks	34,304
	AK	Alaska Regional Office	Natural resource employees professionalization and technical competency enhancement	19,800
	AK	Alaska Regional Office	Produce Alaska Park Science Journal	24,750
	AK	Denali National Park and Preserve	Assess threats to Denali NP&P's class I airshed through comprehensive analysis of long-term data	23,345
	AK	Denali National Park and Preserve	Implement regional integrated pest management (IPM) program to insure health of natural resources	4,727
	AK	Klondike Gold Rush National Historical Park	Contaminants in Alaskan park ecosystem – state of knowledge & gap analysis report	23,500
	AK	Lake Clark National Park and Preserve	Assessing use of marine-derived salmon in wolf diets across Alaskan parks	31,134
	AK	Wrangell-St. Elias National Park and Preserve	Inventory and document bats in Wrangell-St. Elias and Glacier Bay	15,640
IMR	AZ	Pipe Spring National Monument	Implement cooperative study to understand bat ecology of Pipe Spring NM and the Kaibab Paiute Reservation	20,000
	AZ	Saguaro National Park	Mitigate post-flood invasion of tamarisk	40,000
	AZ	Tumacacori National Historical Park	Remove invasive exotic plants from riparian habitat at Tumacacori NHP	20,000
	AZ, UT	Glen Canyon National Recreation Area	Monitor remnant terrace erosion between Glen Canyon Dam and Lees Ferry	10,000
	NM	Pecos National Historical Park	Remove exotic trees to restore Civil War battlefield viewshed	20,000
	NM	White Sands National Monument	The ecology and conservation of the White Sands kit fox	15,130
	TX	Amistad National Recreation Area	Determine breeding success of interior least terns on islands within Lake Amistad Reservoir	20,000
	TX	Big Thicket National Preserve	Restoring native plant communities through partnerships in environmental education	20,000
	WY	Devils Tower National Monument	Control exotic invasive plant species	20,000
MWR	AR	Buffalo National River	Ozark Chinquapin restoration	18,000
	IN	Indiana Dunes National Lakeshore	Restore globally imperiled panne communities	19,000
	MI	Sleeping Bear Dunes National Lakeshore	Increase prairie warbler nesting opportunities through removal of Austrian pine plantation on dunes	21,800
	MN	Voyageurs National Park	Remove exotic invasive species at historic Rainy Lake City, Voyageurs NP	19,000
	MO	Ozark National Scenic Riverways	Quantify white-tailed deer abundance and vegetative impacts within the Big Springs Unit of Ozark NSR	18,000
	MO	Wilson's Creek National Battlefield	Assessing trail use levels and impacts to natural resources	19,000
	NE	Homestead National Monument of America	Improving visitor experience through soundscape management planning	12,550
	NE, SD	Missouri National River and Recreation Area	Determine ecological response to prairie and oak savannah restoration in the Missouri River upland	18,000
	SD	Badlands National Park	Expand park paleontological database to cover the NE corner of the Badlands Wilderness Area	23,110
	WI	Apostle Islands National Lakeshore	Determine the effects of climate change on T&E plant species at Apostle Islands NL	14,000

Table H-4 (cont). NRPP–Regional Program Block projects, FY 2011

Region	State	Park	Project title	FY 2011 funding ($)
NCR	DC	National Capital Parks–East	Analyze data from 5-year monitoring for wetland restoration project	14,200
	DC	National Capital Regional Office	Augmenting and enhancing effective park management of natural resources in NCR	25,000
	DC	National Capital Regional Office	Focusing on educational elements of natural resource research and management	15,300
	DC	National Capital Regional Office	Preserving and restoring natural resources: Field guides for natural vegetation communities	39,000
	DC	Rock Creek Park	Telling the story of the silent green invasion of the meadows in Rock Creek Park	13,700
	MD	Catoctin Mountain Park	Establishing a baseline of critical data impacting brook trout at Catoctin Mountain Park	20,000
	MD	Catoctin Mountain Park	Survey of beetles of Catoctin Mountain Park	18,800
	MD, VA	George Washington Memorial Parkway	Survey of soil invertebrates (earthworms, millipedes, macroarthropods, microarthropods)	20,000
	VA	Prince William Forest Park	Initiate actions recommended by the Isotria Management Plan	20,000
NER	MA	Cape Cod National Seashore	Eradicate phragmites from Herring Pond	5,500
	MA	Cape Cod National Seashore	Complete NEPA Compliance for Shorebird Management	20,000
	ME	Acadia National Park	Develop and test integrated pest management plan for invasive European fire ant	36,500
	NJ, PA	Delaware Water Gap National Recreation Area	Stabilization and sealing of copper mine entrances for bat protection and human safety	45,250
	NY	Fire Island National Seashore	Development of a vegetation management plan	29,036
	NY, PA	Upper Delaware National Scenic and Recreational River	Relative abundance and age structure of adult American shad in the Upper Delaware River	4,500
	VA	Assateague Island National Seashore	Enhance estuarine management through improved sediment analysis	20,000
	VA	Assateague Island National Seashore	Map the distribution and abundance of submerged aquatic vegetation in Assateague Island NS estuarine waters	7,000
	VA	Shenandoah National Park	Eradicate wavyleaf basketgrass	16,354
PWR	AZ	Grand Canyon-Parashant National Monument	Baseline inventory and documentation of cave and karst resources, Grand Canyon-Parashant	45,098
	CA	Sequoia and Kings Canyon National Parks	Restoration of mountain yellow-legged frogs and high mountain lakes and streams in Sequoia and Kings Canyon NPs	25,573
	CA	Sequoia and Kings Canyon National Parks	Restore reed canarygrass-invaded meadows in Grant Grove	30,519
	WA	Mount Rainier National Park	Assessing disease in aquatic breeding amphibian species of concern	35,242
	WA	Mount Rainier National Park	Field-mapping glacier extents at Mount Rainier for hazard recognition	49,484
SER	FL	Canaveral National Seashore	Assess importance of freshwater wetlands to amphibian and reptile biodiversity at Canaveral NS	14,500
	FL	Canaveral National Seashore	Phase II to assess importance of freshwater wetlands to amphibian and reptile biodiversity at Canaveral NS	14,500
	FL	Gulf Islands National Seashore	Determine habitat suitability/restoration needs for wintering resident and migratory songbirds	24,750
	Multiple	Southeast Regional Office	Apply assessment for regional program block allocation	2,511

Table H-4 (cont). NRPP–Regional Program Block projects, FY 2011

Region	State	Park	Project title	FY 2011 funding ($)
SER	NC	Carl Sandburg Home National Historic Site	Eradicate Asiatic dayflower and privet from granitic domes	22,545
	NC, TN	Great Smoky Mountains National Park	Identify and improve fire-dominated bird habitat at Great Smoky Mountains NP	25,000
	SC	Congaree National Park	Assess the magnitude and pattern of floodplain sedimentation in the Bates Fork Tract of Congaree NP	25,000
	SC	Kings Mountain National Military Park	Conduct feasibility study of reintroduction of northern bobwhite quail	25,000
	TN, KY	Big South Fork National Recreation Area	Chemical characterization of native and non-native soil materials from coal mining in Big South Fork NRA	25,000
Other				17,408
TOTAL				1,303,000

Table H-5. NRPP–Regional Small Park Block Allocation projects, FY 2011

Region	State	Park	Project title	FY 2011 funding ($)
AKR	AK	Sitka National Historical Park	Conduct benthic invertebrate and algae investigations to determine biological water quality indexes	9,405
	AK, WA	Klondike Gold Rush National Historical Park	Expand the geographic scope of the western toad monitoring program	9,405
IMR	AZ	Fort Bowie National Historic Site	Apache Spring watershed soil loss reduction and reversal	20,000
	AZ	Pipe Spring National Monument	Monitor groundwater levels for hydrogeologic study of Pipe Spring	4,000
	AZ	Tuzigoot National Monument	Restore wetland plant communities at Tavasci Marsh and vicinity	20,000
	AZ	Walnut Canyon National Monument	Assess the decline of the Arizona walnut population in Walnut Canyon	17,400
	CO	Florissant Fossil Beds National Monument	Invasive weed control and riparian area restoration in Florissant Fossil Beds NM	20,000
	CO	Yucca House National Monument	Landscape protection and restoration at Yucca House NM	20,000
	WY	Devils Tower National Monument	Control exotic invasive plant species and conclude a 50-acre shortgrass meadow restoration	20,000
	MT	Grant-Kohrs Ranch National Historic Site	Evaluate hydrologic function and riparian health of Johnson Creek to develop management options	40,000
	NM	Chaco Culture National Historical Park	Survey, assess condition, and map paleontological resources in Clys Canyon and Mockingbird Areas	19,600
	NM	White Sands National Monument	The ecology and conservation of the White Sands kit fox	8,430
	OK	Chickasaw National Recreation Area	Install gauging station to protect water rights for historic spring district	15,000
	TX	San Antonio Missions National Historical Park	Assess sustainability of state-threatened reptiles	15,150
	UT	Timpanogos Cave National Monument	Restore lower passage environment of Timpanogos Cave	20,000
MWR	AR	Arkansas Post National Memorial	Invasive plant management of disturbed lands	15,000
	AR	Pea Ridge National Military Park	Inventory glades and develop a management plan at Pea Ridge NMP	19,000
	IA	Herbert Hoover National Historic Site	Increase plant diversity in prairie to meet desired conditions established in park general management plan	14,580
	KS	Fort Scott National Historic Site	Conduct a vegetation survey and develop prairie vegetation management plan	16,000
	KS	Tallgrass Prairie National Preserve	Assessment of remote sensing techniques to determine extent of cattle trails in tallgrass prairie	18,000
	MN	Grand Portage National Monument	Conduct experimental forest stand treatments for adaptive restoration management of pine regeneration	20,000
	MN	Grand Portage National Monument	Facilitate boundary resurvey by directing student in the GPS inventory of survey monuments	18,000
	MN	Pipestone National Monument	Implement exotic vegetation control and prairie restoration	12,000
	NE	Homestead National Monument of America	Analyze effectiveness of thicket management at Homestead NM of America	17,000
	SD	Jewel Cave National Monument	Build information base of paleofill sequence to boost future research opportunities	20,400

Table H-5 (cont). NRPP–Regional Small Park Block projects, FY 2011

Region	State	Park	Project title	FY 2011 funding ($)
NCR	DC	National Capital Parks–East	Analyze data from 5-year monitoring for wetland restoration project	3,600
	VA	Manassas National Battlefield Park	Where are the small mammals in Manassas NBP	15,400
NER	MA	Saugus Iron Works National Historic Site	Control non-native trees in riparian forest	30,000
	ME	Acadia National Park	Develop and test integrated pest management plan for invasive European fire ant	8,387
	Multiple	Northeast Regional Office	Natural resource technical assistance	24,922
	PA	Allegheny Portage Railroad National Historic Site	Control hemlock woolly adelgid at Allegheny Portage hemlock and hardwood stands 2011	2,965
	PA	Valley Forge National Historical Park	An evaluation of existing vegetation data and data gaps leading to inventories and forest management	20,166
	PA	Valley Forge National Historical Park	Reconstruction of 'public' deer exclosure at Valley Forge NHP	9,500
	PA	Valley Forge National Historical Park	Restoration of warm-season grasslands on recently acquired property at Valley Forge NHP	11,900
	VA	Appomattox Court House National Historical Park	Apply herbicide to control privet	7,000
PWR	American Samoa	National Park of American Samoa	Reduce and control the most destructive invasive tree in National Park of American Samoa: *Falcataria moluccana*	26,608
	AZ	Grand Canyon-Parashant National Monument	Baseline inventory and documentation of cave and karst resources, Grand Canyon-Parashant	1,229
	AZ	Grand Canyon-Parashant National Monument	Inventory and analysis of fossil resources found within KyPet Caverns	1,897
	AZ	Grand Canyon-Parashant National Monument	Tamarisk treatment and restoration of newly identified invasions at 7 springs on Grand Canyon-Parashant	25,000
	CA	Lava Beds National Monument	Protect bighorn sheep paleo resources	7,000
	CA	Lava Beds National Monument	Remove 3500' of trail base identified as a serious threat to lava tube ecosystems	22,195
	ID	Craters of the Moon National Monument and Preserve	Woad be gone; attacking a new invader	30,000
	OR, WA	Lewis and Clark National Historical Park	Noxious weed control on recently acquired farm and forest tracts	19,771
	OR, WA	Lewis and Clark National Historical Park	Restoration of recently acquired coastal forest and dunes	1,300
	WA	San Juan Island National Historical Park	Update vegetation management plan	26,000
SER	GA	Kings Mountain National Military Park	Monitor and retreat exotic plant populations to maintain wildlife habitat and conserve scenery	25,000
	GA, TN	Chickamauga and Chattanooga National Military Park	Control non-native invasive plants within the Chickamauga and Chattanooga NMP	12,704
	MS	Vicksburg National Military Park	Exclude and relocate bats from Illinois Monument	24,722
	Multiple	Southeast Regional Office	Resource stewardship strategy implementation	14,637
	NC	Carl Sandburg Home National Historic Site	Conserve culturally and botanically significant plants of Carl Sandburg Home NHS	23,857
	SC	Congaree National Park	Implement feral hog control at Congaree NP	24,997

Table H-5 (cont). NRPP–Regional Small Park Block projects, FY 2011

Region	State	Park	Project title	FY 2011 funding ($)
	TN	Obed Wild and Scenic River	Bank-operated cableway for streamflow and water quality measurement in the Obed WSR	25,000
	TN	Stones River National Battlefield	Stones River floodplain restoration	24,809
	USVI	Virgin Islands Coral Reef National Monument	Habitat protection and resource access in Virgin Islands Coral Reef NM, phase III	15,200
Other				18,864
TOTAL				933,000

Table H-6. NRPP–Servicewide projects, FY 2011

Program	Project title	FY 2011 funding ($)
Biological Resource Management	2011 bioblitz discovery events	120,000
Biological Resource Management	Review of NPS ungulate management	50,000
Geologic Resources	Solar PEIS geospatial evaluation	43,000
NRSS	Benefits sharing agreement support	31,000
NRSS	Cosponsor support, NAA conference	2,500
NRSS	Director's natural resource awards	47,000
NRSS	Modernization of NPS Research Permit and Reporting System	160,000
NRSS	Park Science	20,000
NRSS	Renewable energy development	200,000
NRSS	Report to Congress	8,000
NRSS	Ungulate management, Channel Islands NP	100,000
Water Resources	Invasive lionfish response plan workshop	20,000
TOTAL[a]		801,500

[a] $22,500 in NRPP funds were reallocated from Natural Resource Management to Servicewide projects to complete their obligation at the close of FY 2011.

Table H-7. NRPP–Threatened and Endangered Species projects, FY 2011

Region	State	Park	Project title	FY 2011 funding ($)
IMR	TX	Big Bend National Park	Protect threatened Chisos hedgehog cactus from exotic grass invasion	20,790
	WY	Glacier National Park	Preservation of threatened bull trout in Glacier NP	42,570
	AZ, UT	Glen Canyon National Recreation Area	Create a protected nursery to expand populations of endangered Colorado River native fish	9,900
	CO	Rocky Mountain National Park	Determine the distribution of greenback cutthroat trout in Rocky Mountain NP	45,540
MWR	MO	Ozark National Scenic Riverways	Determine summer habitat use by Indiana bats to inform adaptive management actions at Ozark NSR	48,510
NCR	VA	Prince William Forest Park	Restore the federally threatened small-whorled pogonia in three NPS regions	50,000
PWR	CA	Golden Gate National Recreation Area	Enhance habitat for Golden Gate NRA mission blue butterfly through habitat disturbance actions	81,000
	HI	Hawaii Volcanoes National Park	Re-establish endangered *Clermontia peleana* on the Island of Hawaii	61,000
	WA	Olympic National Park	Protect and restore ESA-listed fish during removal of the Elwha River dams	75,000
	CA	Pinnacles National Monument	Restoring California condors at Pinnacles NM: Use of isotopes to identify sources of lead poisoning	5,000
SER	NC, TN	Great Smoky Mountains National Park	Determine habitat requirements and survey for federally endangered spruce-fir moss spider in Great Smoky Mountains NP	13,811
Other				1,879
TOTAL[a]				455,000

[a]The total reflects $12,000 reallocated between the Golden Gate NRA and Pinnacles NM projects funded through Threatened and Endangered Species and the Point Reyes NS Scotch broom project funded through Natural Resource Management.

Appendix I: Park-Oriented Biological Support (POBS) Projects

Table I-1. Park-Oriented Biological Support (POBS) Projects, FY 2011

Region	State	Park	Project title
IMR	CO	Great Sand Dunes National Park and Preserve	Developing a grazing monitoring program for Great Sand Dunes NP, Colorado
	CO	Rocky Mountain National Park	Identifying and implementing a quantitative approach to measuring success in boreal toad reintroductions
	MT	Glacier National Park	Assessing the threat of climate change to headwater amphibians in Glacier NP
	MT	Glacier National Park	Maximizing legacy databases to understand climate change effects on alpine vegetation[a]
	TX	Padre Island National Seashore	Ecological importance of biodiversity hotspots to coastal sharks: Characterizing apex predator usage of Padre Island NS
	WY, MT, ID	Yellowstone National Park	Effects of sarcoptic mange on gray wolves in Yellowstone NP
MWR	MI	Sleeping Bear Dunes National Seashore	Algal benthic invertebrate community as a source of bird botulism pathogen
	NE	Niobrara National Scenic River	Past and present tree density in Niobrara Valley forest: Implications for managing paper birch populations
	SD	Badlands National Park	Pollination webs to guide management of rare and invasive species in a changing climate
PWR	CA	Channel Islands National Park	Development of a monitoring framework for the island scrub-jay
	CA	Sequoia and Kings Canyon National Parks	Designing a giant sequoia monitoring program
	CA	Yosemite National Park	The effects of fire severity on California spotted owl habitat use in a burned landscape in Yosemite NP, California
	CA	Yosemite National Park, Lassen Volcanic National Park, Sequoia and Kings Canyon National Parks, Devils Postpile National Monument	Impact of climate change on future suitability of the Sierra Nevada for wolverines[a]
	CA	Yosemite National Park, Sequoia and Kings Canyon National Parks	Determining the ages and carbon storage rates of Sierra Nevada fens
	CA	Yosemite National Park, Sequoia and Kings Canyon National Parks	Integrating early detection and control of velvetgrass (*Holcus lanatus*) in Yosemite and Sequoia and Kings Canyon NPs
	ID	City of Rocks National Reserve	Vegetation and fire history of City of Rocks National Reserve: Relevance for understanding the role of climate and disturbance in plant migration in the American West[a]
	OR, ID	Crater Lake National Park, Craters of the Moon National Monument and Preserve	Developing genetic-based connectivity models for the American pika
	WA	Olympic National Park	Evaluate fisher restoration in Olympic NP
SER	TN	Great Smoky Mountains National Park	Identifying the appropriate unit of management for Great Smoky Mountains NP brook trout (*Salvelinus fontinalis*)
	Virgin Islands	Virgin Islands Coral Reef National Monument	Exploring the links between coral reefs and mangroves: Characterization of Hurricane Hole, Virgin Islands Coral Reef NM[a]

[a]Project received climate change funding.

Park Index

A

Acadia National Park 11, 39, 40, 53, 60, 61, 73, 76
Alagnak Wild River 24, 64
Allegheny Portage Railroad National Historic Site 76
Amistad National Recreation Area 26, 70, 72
Aniakchak National Monument and Preserve 64
Antietam National Battlefield 34, 37, 53
Apostle Islands National Lakeshore 30, 62, 72
Appalachian National Scenic Trail 38, 53
Appomattox Court House National Historical Park 76
Arches National Park 60
Arkansas Post National Memorial 30, 75
Assateague Island National Seashore 16, 69, 73

B

Badlands National Park 30, 31, 33, 49, 70, 72, 79
Bandelier National Monument 64, 70
Big Bend National Park 15, 64, 66, 70, 78
Big Cypress National Preserve 45, 46, 53, 65
Bighorn Canyon National Recreation Area 64, 70
Big South Fork National River and Recreation Area 15, 16, 45, 71
Big Thicket National Preserve 60, 72
Black Canyon of the Gunnison National Park 50, 59, 64
Blue Ridge Parkway 50, 71
Booker T Washington National Monument 64
Boston Harbor Islands National Recreation Area 39
Buck Island Reef National Monument 45, 53
Buffalo National River 13, 68, 69, 72

C

Canaveral National Seashore 46, 73
Canyonlands National Park 16, 60
Cape Cod National Seashore 19, 38, 39, 40, 62, 66, 73
Cape Hatteras National Seashore 14, 16, 65
Cape Lookout National Seashore 14, 16, 65
Capitol Reef National Park 29, 60
Carl Sandburg Home National Historic Site 65, 74, 76
Carlsbad Caverns National Park 59
Catoctin Mountain Park 34, 35, 37, 53, 64, 73
Chaco Culture National Historical Park 26, 75
Channel Islands National Park 53, 61, 66, 69, 70, 77, 79
Chattahoochee River National Recreation Area 65
Chesapeake and Ohio Canal National Historical Park 34, 64, 70
Chickamauga and Chattanooga National Military Park 76
Chickasaw National Recreation Area 75
City of Rocks National Reserve 79
Congaree National Park 10, 59, 61, 65, 74, 76
Coronado National Memorial 53
Crater Lake National Park 60, 63, 64, 79
Craters of the Moon National Monument and Preserve 60, 76, 79
Cumberland Gap National Historical Park 50
Cumberland Island National Seashore 65, 71
Curecanti National Recreation Area 53, 64
Cuyahoga Valley National Park 62

D

Death Valley National Park 62, 64, 66
Delaware Water Gap National Recreation Area 38, 50, 73
Denali National Park and Preserve 17, 24, 59, 69, 72
Devils Postpile National Monument 43, 79
Devils Tower National Monument 72, 75
Dinosaur National Monument 19, 26, 27, 53, 65, 66
Dry Tortugas National Park 71

E

Everglades National Park 61, 65

F

Fire Island National Seashore 39, 40, 70, 73
Florissant Fossil Beds National Monument 75
Fort Bowie National Historic Site 75
Fort Matanzas National Monument 16, 47
Fort Scott National Historic Site 75
Fossil Butte National Monument 29
Fredericksburg & Spotsylvania National Military Park 6, 64

G

Gates of the Arctic National Park and Preserve 53
Gateway National Recreation Area 39
George Washington Birthplace National Monument 4
George Washington Memorial Parkway 73
Glacier Bay National Park and Preserve 24, 25, 68, 69, 70
Glacier National Park 4, 26, 50, 60, 61, 62, 69, 78, 79

Upper Kijik River valley, Lake Clark National Park and Preserve, Alaska
NPS/DAN YOUNG

Glen Canyon National Recreation Area 14, 18, 60, 72, 78
Golden Gate National Recreation Area 14, 16, 41, 42, 60, 63, 67, 69, 78
Golden Spike National Historic Site 29
Grand Canyon National Park 50, 60, 69
Grand Canyon-Parashant National Monument 5, 73, 76
Grand Portage National Monument 64, 75
Grand Teton National Park 11, 19, 27, 50, 60, 66, 69, 70
Grant-Kohrs Ranch National Historic Site 75
Great Basin National Park 50, 53, 66
Great Sand Dunes National Park and Preserve 12, 27, 53, 60, 79
Great Smoky Mountains National Park 11, 38, 45, 46, 50, 53, 68, 71, 74, 78, 79
Guadalupe Mountains National Park 59, 64
Gulf Islands National Seashore 8, 16, 61, 73

H

Haleakala National Park 53, 61, 63, 71
Harpers Ferry National Historical Park 35
Hawaii Volcanoes National Park 11, 12, 61, 63, 64, 78
Herbert Hoover National Historic Site 31, 75
Homestead National Monument of America 53, 72, 75
Hopewell Culture National Historical Park 31, 53
Horseshoe Bend National Military Park 65
Hot Springs National Park 31

I

Indiana Dunes National Lakeshore 9, 16, 72
Isle Royale National Park 59

J

Jean Lafitte National Historical Park and Preserve 62
Jefferson National Expansion Memorial 14
Jewel Cave National Monument 31, 53, 75
John Day Fossil Beds National Monument 53, 62
Joshua Tree National Park 44, 60, 64

K

Kalaupapa National Historical Park 19, 41, 53, 61, 66
Kaloko-Honokōhau National Historical Park 14, 19, 49, 61, 65, 66
Katmai National Park and Preserve 24, 25, 59, 64
Kenai Fjords National Park 25, 69, 70
Kennesaw Mountain National Battlefield Park 65
Kings Mountain National Military Park 74, 76

Klondike Gold Rush National Historical Park 72, 75
Kobuk Valley National Park 25

L

Lake Clark National Park and Preserve 23, 24, 53, 69, 72, 81
Lake Mead National Recreation Area 60, 64, 66
Lake Meredith National Recreation Area 14
Lassen Volcanic National Park 12, 60, 64, 79
Lava Beds National Monument 49, 60, 64, 76
Lewis and Clark National Historical Park 76
Lewis and Clark National Historic Trail 62
Little Bighorn Battlefield National Monument 64
Little River Canyon National Preserve 46, 53

M

Mammoth Cave National Park 11, 46, 47, 68, 71
Manassas National Battlefield Park 37, 76
Mesa Verde National Park 61
Missouri National River and Recreation Area 72
Mojave National Preserve 53, 60, 64
Monocacy National Battlefield 35, 37, 53
Moores Creek National Battlefield 65
Mount Rainier National Park 59, 63, 64, 73
Mount Rushmore National Memorial 50

N

National Capital Parks–East 35, 73, 76
National Park of American Samoa 61, 70, 76
New River Gorge National River iii, 40, 50, 70
Nez Perce National Historical Park 65
Niobrara National Scenic River 79
North Cascades National Park ii, 1, 62, 64

O

Obed Wild and Scenic River 50, 53, 77
Ocmulgee National Monument 65
Olympic National Park 49, 61, 63, 71, 78, 79
Organ Pipe Cactus National Monument 28, 70
Ozark National Scenic Riverways 72, 78

P

Padre Island National Seashore 53, 59, 64, 79
Palo Alto Battlefield National Historical Park 3
Pea Ridge National Military Park 32, 75
Pecos National Historical Park 16, 72
Petersburg National Battlefield 64
Petrified Forest National Park 68
Petroglyph National Monument 64
Pictured Rocks National Lakeshore 32, 53, 59, 68
Pinnacles National Monument 41, 42, 70, 71, 78
Pipe Springs National Monument 72, 75

Pipestone National Monument 75
Point Reyes National Seashore 4, 14, 42, 49, 71
Prince William Forest Park 35, 73, 78
Pu'uhonua o Hōnaunau National Historical Park 42
Pu'ukoholā Heiau National Historic Site 14, 49

R
Redwood National and State Parks 60
Rock Creek Park 14, 35, 36, 37, 53, 73
Rocky Mountain National Park 11, 12, 28, 50, 57, 60, 61, 62, 64, 78, 79

S
Saguaro National Park 4, 12, 28, 59, 70, 72
Saint Croix National Scenic Riverway 64
San Antonio Missions National Historical Park 75
Sand Creek Massacre National Historic Site 64
San Juan Island National Historical Park 43, 53, 76
Santa Monica Mountains National Recreation Area 60, 62, 71
Saugus Iron Works National Historic Site 39, 53, 76
Sequoia and Kings Canyon National Parks 11, 14, 43, 53, 60, 69, 73, 79
Shenandoah National Park 11, 35, 38, 50, 60, 73
Sitka National Historical Park 25, 75
Sleeping Bear Dunes National Lakeshore 21, 33, 61, 68, 70, 72
Stones River National Battlefield 53, 71, 77
Sunset Crater National Monument 53

T
Tallgrass Prairie National Preserve 75
Theodore Roosevelt National Park 32, 53, 62, 70
Timpanogos Cave National Monument 4, 28, 29, 75
Timucuan Ecological and Historic Preserve 65
Tumacacori National Historical Park 72
Tuzigoot National Monument 75

U
Upper Delaware National Scenic and Recreational River 73

V
Valley Forge National Historical Park 76
Vicksburg National Military Park 76
Virgin Islands Coral Reef National Monument 66, 77, 79
Virgin Islands National Park 53, 66
Voyageurs National Park 64, 72

W
Walnut Canyon National Monument 53, 75
Washita Battlefield National Historic Site 64
Whiskeytown National Recreation Area 43, 68, 69
White Sands National Monument 15, 18, 19, 66, 72, 75
Wind Cave National Park 60, 66, 67, 70
Wolf Trap National Park for the Performing Arts 37
World War II Valor in the Pacific National Monument 17
Wrangell-St. Elias National Park and Preserve 12, 25, 69, 70, 72
Wupatki National Monument 53

Y
Yellowstone National Park 14, 27, 51, 60, 61, 79
Yosemite National Park 11, 12, 43, 60, 61, 64, 65, 79
Yucca House National Monument 75

Z
Zion National Park 28, 53, 60, 63, 64

State and Territory Index

A
Alabama 46, 65
Alaska iii, 4, 9, 12, 17, 19, 20, 23, 24, 25, 50, 56, 57, 59, 60, 61, 64, 66, 68, 69, 70, 72, 75, 81, 86
American Samoa 61, 70, 76, 82
Arizona 4, 5, 12, 14, 17, 18, 28, 50, 59, 64, 66, 68, 69, 70, 72, 73, 75, 76, 78
Arkansas 13, 30, 31, 32, 69, 72, 75, 81, 82

C
California 4, 9, 11, 12, 14, 16, 28, 41, 42, 43, 44, 46, 49, 60, 61, 62, 64, 65, 66, 67, 68, 69, 70, 71, 73, 76, 78, 79
Colorado 4, 11, 12, 19, 26, 27, 28, 49, 50, 55, 57, 59, 61, 62, 64, 66, 75, 78, 79

D
District of Columbia i, 14, 34, 35, 36, 37, 62, 64, 70, 73, 76, 88

F
Florida 4, 8, 16, 45, 46, 47, 55, 57, 60, 61, 65, 71, 73

G
Georgia 38, 65, 71, 76

H
Hawaii 4, 11, 12, 14, 17, 19, 41, 42, 49, 50, 55, 61, 63, 64, 65, 66, 71, 78, 82

I
Idaho 14, 27, 51, 65, 76, 79
Indiana 9, 16, 38, 60, 72, 78, 82
Iowa 31, 75

K
Kansas 75
Kentucky 11, 16, 45, 46, 47, 50, 68, 71, 74

L
Louisiana 62

M
Maine 11, 38, 39, 60, 61, 73, 76
Maryland 4, 16, 34, 35, 37, 64, 69, 70, 73
Massachusetts 19, 38, 39, 40, 62, 66, 73, 76
Michigan 21, 32, 33, 59, 61, 68, 70, 72, 79
Mississippi 61, 76
Missouri 14, 72, 78
Montana 4, 14, 26, 27, 50, 51, 60, 61, 62, 64, 69, 70, 75, 79

N
Nebraska 31, 53, 72, 75, 79
Nevada 50, 64, 66
New Jersey 38, 50, 73
New Mexico 15, 16, 18, 19, 26, 59, 64, 66, 70, 71, 72, 75, 77, 78
New York 39, 40, 70, 73
North Carolina 11, 14, 16, 38, 46, 50, 65, 68, 71, 74, 76, 78
North Dakota 32, 62, 67, 70

O
Ohio 31, 62
Oklahoma 64, 75
Oregon 62, 63, 64, 76, 79

P
Pennsylvania 50, 73, 76

S
South Carolina 10, 59, 61, 65, 74, 76
South Dakota 30, 31, 33, 49, 50, 60, 66, 67, 70, 72, 75, 79

T
Tennessee 11, 15, 16, 38, 45, 46, 50, 68, 71, 74, 76, 77, 78, 79
Texas 3, 14, 15, 26, 59, 60, 64, 66, 70, 72, 75, 78, 79

U
Utah 4, 14, 16, 18, 26, 27, 28, 29, 63, 64, 65, 66, 72, 75, 78

V
Virginia iii, 4, 6, 11, 16, 35, 37, 38, 40, 50, 60, 64, 69, 73, 76, 78
Virgin Islands 45, 53, 66, 77, 79, 83

W
Washington ii, i, 1, 3, 4, 9, 15, 43, 44, 49, 59, 61, 62, 63, 64, 71, 73, 75, 76, 78, 79, 81, 88
West Virginia iii, 34, 35, 40, 50, 64, 70
Wisconsin 30, 62, 64, 72
Wyoming 11, 14, 19, 27, 29, 50, 51, 64, 66, 69, 70, 72, 75, 78, 79

The Department of the Interior protects and manages the nation's natural resources and cultural heritage; provides scientific and other information about those resources; and honors its special responsibilities to American Indians, Alaska Natives, and affiliated Island Communities.

NPS 909/115244, June 2012

www.ingramcontent.com/pod-product-compliance
Lightning Source LLC
Chambersburg PA
CBHW081834170526
45167CB00007B/2801